I0005903

CONTENTS

PREFACE

In the dark ages, only those with power or great wealth (and selected experts) possessed reading and writing skills or the ability to acquire them. It can be argued that literacy of the general population (while still not 100%), together with the invention of printing technology, has been one of the most emancipatory forces of modern history.

We have only recently entered the information age, and it is expected that computer and communication technology will soon replace printing as the dominant form of information distribution technology. About half of all US households already own at least one personal computer, and this number is still growing.

However, while many people nowadays use a computer, few of them are computer programmers. Non-programmers aren't really "empowered" in how they can use their computer: they are confined to using applications in ways that "programmers" have determined for them. One doesn't need to be a visionary to see the limitations here.

An even more radical change is the introduction of computing and communications embedded in home and office systems. The number of devices that will contain programmable elements is expected to grow dramatically in the coming years. We must learn how to expose this programmability to users in a meaningful way and to make it easy for non-programmers to control and program these devices.

In this "expedition into the future," we want to explore the notion that virtually everybody can obtain *some* level of computer programming skills in school, just as they can learn how to read and write.

There are many challenges for programming languages and environments to be used by a mass audience. If everybody is a programmer, poor programmers will surely abound. Coping with this situation adequately requires a rethinking of the fundamental properties of programming languages and development tools. Yet, we believe that there should be no clear-cut distinction between tools used by professionals and tools used for education--just as professional writers use the same language and alphabet as their readers!

Given the ever more pervasive use of computers and software in every aspect of society, we expect the need for programming skills will only increase. While most quality software will be produced by professionals, there will be a need for more programming and customizability by end users.

Examples of this drive for flexibility can be seen in both present-day computing and its likely future:

- Increasingly powerful applications for desktop and laptop computers use scripting and macro facilities.
- Growth of the Internet has led directly to greater need for programmability to create active and interactive Web content.

- End-user information appliances and networks of CPUs embedded in everyday objects--both will demand user control and personalization.
- Mobile and intelligent software agents will be commonplace and require customization by users.

In the future, we envision that computer programming will be taught in elementary school, just like reading, writing and arithmetic. We really mean computer *programming*--not just computer use (which is already being taught). Of course, most children won't grow up to be skilled application developers, just as most people don't become professional authors--but reading and writing skills are useful for everyone, and so (in our vision) will be general programming skills. For the time being, we set our goals a bit less ambitious. We focus on teaching programming to high school and (non-CS major) college undergraduates. If we are successful here, we expect that the lower grades will soon follow, within their limitations.

In addition to the goal of teaching how computers work, a course in computer programming will return to the curriculum an emphasis on logical thought which was once the main benefit of teaching geometry.

Two general computing trends of particular interest are the move towards information appliances and the growth of embedded CPUs in everyday machines and appliances-- whether in the military or the civilian sector. The decreasing size of computing and the increasing reach of networking, particularly wireless networking, make it possible to share information between devices and to interact with them. The ability to program will greatly improve users' ability to control these devices. Imagine that users could make their own changes to the software embedded in, say, their GPS receiver or handheld organizer, rather than (or in addition to) downloading upgrades from a vendor or buying "canned" add-on applications from third parties. This would greatly empower people to improve their life by programming their personal tools to do exactly what they need them to do.

If we are successful, non-experts will be able use their computers and other intelligent devices much more effectively, reducing their level of frustration and increasing their productivity and work satisfaction. (New leisure possibilities will undoubtedly ensue as well!) Computer users will be able to solve their own computer problems more often, reducing the need for technical support.

Even if most users do not program regularly, a familiarity with programming and the structure of software will make them more effective users of computers. For example, when something goes wrong, they will be able to make a better mental model of the likely failure, which will allow them to fix or work around the problem. They will also be able to assess better when they can make the changes themselves and when they will need the services of an expert. They will be more able to converse with experts, since they will now share more of a common language. An analogy is obtaining basic literacy in automotive maintenance: you know enough to check your oil and add a few quarts if necessary, but you also know that you shouldn't try to change your own brakes. When the mechanic says "your rotors are warped and you need new pads," you understand what he is talking about.

If this effort is successful, there could be many millions, eventually billions of computer programmers, at various levels of proficiency. The effects this will have on the state of the art of software development is hard to imagine. The nature of software will change to accommodate the needs of these programmers, allowing customization through source code modifications--and personalizations will be plentiful.

The effort could also have a major impact on getting women and minorities into computer programming--currently, these groups are vastly underrepresented.

The recently popular open source movement [OpenSource] is promising to improve the quality of key software packages through the peer review of thousands, as well as the ability for programmers to "scratch their own itch" (i.e., tweak the software in a minor way that only one individual cares about). We expect that moving from thousands to millions or billions of programmers will further change the nature of the software development process. Personal programming will become more important (and feasible) at this scale, while mass peer review will become relatively less important, due to diminished returns (the logistics of integrating bug fixes from thousands of sources is already a formidable task). But most current software, open source or otherwise, is too complex to allow anyone to do personal customization without first investing a serious amount of effort and time into understanding the software they're using. We are interested in changes to the whole software development process that will fix this as well--in particular, development tools.

In addition, by enabling the programmability of applications by anybody, we will leverage economies of scale without sacrificing the desire of users for highly personalized software. Applications can be mass-produced, without forcing everyone to fit the same mold in their use of the software (or into just those eddies of customizability planned by the developers). Users will want to personalize their systems for a number of reasons; these include becoming more productive, solving a problem peculiar to their needs, or just expressing their creativity and setting themselves apart from their peers. They will be able to achieve this if they have the basic programming literacy we envision.

Some broad questions help frame our specific research goals, such as: Will the programming language taught in schools resemble the programming languages we know today? Will it even be called a programming language? How will we teach it? Will there be only one language? What other tools are essential to the teaching and use of this language? Is it even possible to have a language and tools that are both good for teaching and useful for experts?

Just as interesting are questions like these: How and for what purposes will people use their programming skills? How will a near-universal ability to read and write computer programs change the structure and utility of computer software? (This is especially interesting in combination with future versions of the Internet, which promise high-speed ubiquitous access to computing and storage elements.) Will people be motivated to actually program their systems once they have the confidence that they can? Will they even be interested in the first place?

A clear concern is the expectation that, if most people are programmers, many of them will most likely be *poor* programmers. People who can't write understandable sentences in their native tongue or balance their checkbook are unlikely to write well-structured computer programs! Our intent, however, is to make programming accessible, if not easy, for

4

everyone. Some users will employ or contract a third party programming and customization service. This is much like a homeowner contracting out for a remodeling job.

We therefore need to investigate ways to improve the quality of the interaction between the programmer and the system, to help even poor programmers get the most out of their computers. For example, you might want to write a program to customize your PDA or toaster, but you might be discouraged if a small mistake could wipe out your address book or set your house on fire. Safeguards against disasters are needed, as well as ways of backing out of unwanted changes to a system as a whole. ("Undo", while very powerful, usually only applies to one file at a time. Backing out of unwanted global system changes typically requires a reboot or even painful data restoration from back-up media.)

Another concern regards configuration management. Without superior configuration management, businesses are going to find themselves either unable to correct problems, or held hostage by programmers who have modified the operating system or applications in a manner that precludes either upgrading or making other changes. In general, all locally made changes to large software systems are currently in danger of being incompatible with future upgrades of the primary product. Even locally produced software may be rendered unusable when the primary developer leaves, due to a number of reasons including lack of testing or documentation.

Apart from the fear that something might go wrong, another concern for beginning programmers who are interested in customizing their computer is the daunting task of trying to understand a large piece of existing software. We need to look into user-friendly tools for program analysis; more about this later. Another intellectual challenge is visualization of (application-generated) data in ways that help novices. Spreadsheets are of great value here, but not all data fits the matrix form.

Scripting languages are growing in popularity among professional programmers [Ousterhout], but questions remain about performance, software reuse, and integration with components written in other languages. We can address these challenges by enhancing the facilities of JPython [Hugunin1], a Python dialect seamlessly integrated with Java, and SWIG, an interface generator that creates interfaces between scripting languages and systems languages like C or C++.

Why Teach a "General" Programming Language?

It is well understood that there is something of a dichotomy between "general" programming languages on the one hand and "domain-specific" languages on the other. For this discussion, we use the term "general" in a broad and loose sense, to include functional programming languages and possibly even logic programming languages, to the extent to which they are usable as a general programming tool. Turing-completeness is the key concept here.

The domain-specific category then contains everything else, from command line argument syntax to email headers and HTML. The distinguishing factor here is the presence of a relatively narrow application domain. In this category we also place things like Microsoft's "wizards" (really just sequences of predefined dialogs connected by simple flow charts) and the controls and dials on microwave ovens or nuclear reactors.

A typical property of domain-specific languages is that they provide excellent control in the application domain for which they were intended, and (almost) no freedom in unanticipated areas. For example, HTML has no inherent ability for conditional inclusion of text, or for variable expansion. (The fact that such features have been added many times as incompatible extensions merely proves this point.)

General languages, on the other hand, usually aren't as good in any particular domain. For example, it is much harder to write a program in a general language to format a paragraph of text than it is in HTML. However, general languages make up for this through their Turing-completeness, which makes it possible to solve *any* problem that might come up (assuming availability of sufficient resources). General languages are therefore ideal when used in *combination* with domain-specific languages.

For example, if cell phones were programmable, one would still use the regular domain-specific interface (the keypad) to dial a specific number, since that's the most convenient way to access that specific functionality. However, without programmability, there is no way to make it try several different numbers for a particular friend until one is answered, unless the cell phone vendor anticipated this particular feature.

Why Start with Python?

We propose to start by making it possible to teach programming in Python, an existing scripting language, and to focus on creating a new development environment and teaching materials for it. We have anecdotal evidence that Python is a good language to teach as a first programming language. Our effort will focus on creating tools and educational materials for this purpose and on fostering a community around those materials. This will allow us to study in what ways Python is a good (or bad) language for teaching, and instigate directions for future development.

Why start with an existing language? Our experience indicates that the design and implementation of a new language takes years--and that this work must be (nearly) completed before a user-friendly development environment and teaching materials can be created. So we jump-start by using an existing language.

We already have some evidence of where changes might be necessary. Prof. Randy Pausch at Carnegie Mellon University (see below) has conducted some usability studies of Python within their limited problem domain. Their users seemed most confused by the case sensitivity of Python's variable names and by the truncation of integer division. More extensive and generalized studies will serve to drive specific changes to Python, or indicate the need for a newly designed language.

Python is a good language for teaching absolute beginners. It derives many of its critical features from ABC, a language that was designed specifically for teaching programming to non-experts [ABC] [Geurts]. The Python community has seen many reports from individuals who taught their children programming using Python. The consensus from these reports is that the language itself is well suited for this purpose--unlike, for example, C++, Java, Perl, Tcl, or Visual Basic, which are too cluttered with idiosyncrasies.

Python is a good *first choice* for teaching which also serves well as a language for more serious application development. Unlike other languages proposed for teaching to novices (e.g. Logo, LogoMation, even Python's ancestor ABC), Python isn't *just* a teaching language. It is suitable for developing large real applications elsewhere. For example, Industrial Light and Magic has converted its entire tool base to Python and considers this an advantage over the competition.

Moreover, Python is extensible by modules written in other languages (e.g. C, C++, or Java), to mediate access to advanced functionality that is not easily accessible from Python directly (for example, high-speed 3-D computer graphics packages). While we don't expect students to write these extension modules, the *use* of such modules makes it possible to spruce up their learning experience greatly. This extensibility gives teachers an opportunity to tailor lessons to the interests of their students by providing them with guarded access to other software packages.

This book is intended for students and other computing professionals who are new to Python but want to learn this interactive language. With the help of interesting and easy to read learning tutorials they will be able to grasp the core concepts of this language and will not only master the skills of python language but will start thinking like Computer Scientists in just 10 days.

DAY-1

PYTHON SYNTAX

Welcome to the Flying Circus

Python is a powerful, flexible programming language you can use in web/Internet development, to write desktop graphical user interfaces (GUIs), create games, and much more. Python is:

• **High-level**, meaning reading and writing Python is really easy—it looks a lot like regular English!

• **Interpreted**, meaning you don't need a compiler to write and run Python! You can write it on your own computer (many are shipped with the Python **interpreter** built in—we'll get to the interpreter later in this lesson).

• **Object-oriented**, meaning it allows users to manipulate data structures called **objects** in order to build and execute programs. We'll learn more about objects later.

• **Fun to use**. Python is named after *Monty Python's Flying Circus*, and example code and tutorials often refer to the show and include jokes in order to make learning the language more interesting.

This course assumes no previous knowledge of Python in particular or programming/computer science in general.

Variables

One of the most basic concepts in computer programming is the **variable**. A variable is a word/identifier that hangs onto a single **value**. For example, let's say you needed the number 5for your program, but you're not going to use it immediately. You can set a variable, say spam, to grab the value 5 and hang onto it for later use, like this:

```
spam = 5
```

Declaring variables in Python is easy; you just write out a name/identifier, like spam, and use = to assign it a value, and you're done!

Instruction:

Now set the variable my_variable to the value 10 as shown in Figure below:

```
script.py

1  # Write your code below!
2  submit=3
3  my_variable=10
```

Data Types

Great! We can now summon the value `10` by calling out the name `my_variable` whenever we need it.

In this case, the **data type** of `my_variable` is an **integer** (a positive or negative whole number). There are three data types in Python that are of interest to us at the moment: integers (**int** in Python language), **floats** (fractional numbers written with a decimal point, like `1.970`), and **booleans** (which can be `True` or `False`).

Computer programs, in large part, are created to manipulate data. Therefore, it's important to understand the different types of data (or "datatypes") that we can incorporate into our programs.

Never use quotation marks (' or ") with booleans, and always capitalize the first letter! Python is **case-sensitive** (it cares about capitalization). We'll use quotation marks when we get to **strings**, which we'll cover in the next unit.

Instruction:

Now set the following variables to the corresponding values as shown in Figure below:

1. my_int to the value 7

2. my_float to the value 1.23
3. my_bool to the value True

```
script.py

1   # Set the variables to the values listed in the instructions!
2   my_int=7
3   my_float=1.23
4   my_bool=True
```

You've Been Reassigned

Great work. You now know how to declare variables in Python and set them to different values, and you've learned about three different types of values: integers, floats, and booleans.

You can reassign a variable at any point. If you first set `my_int` to 7 but later want to change it to 3, all you have to do is tell Python `my_int = 3`, and it'll change the value of `my_int` for you.

Instruction:

Change the value of my_int from 7 to 3 in the editor as shown in Figure below:

```
script.py

1    # my_int is set to 7 below. What do you think
2    # will happen if we reset it to 3 and print the result?
3
4    my_int = 7
5
6    # Change the value of my_int to 3 on line 8!
7
8    my_int =3
9
10 - # Here's some code that will print my_int to the console:
11   # The print keyword will be covered in detail soon!
12
13   print my_int
```

What's a Statement?

You can think of a Python **statement** as being similar to a sentence in English: it's the smallest unit of the language that makes sense by itself. Just like "I," "like," and "Spam" aren't sentences by themselves, but "I like Spam" *is*, variables and data types aren't statements in Python, but they *are* the building blocks that form them.

To continue the sentence analogy, it's clear that we also need a kind of punctuation to make it obvious where one statement ends and another begins. If you're familiar with JavaScript, you know that statements end with a semicolon (;). In Python, statements are separated by **whitespace**. Just like you can't toss around semicolons wherever you want in JS, you can't throw whitespace around in Python.

This may take some getting used to, especially if you're coming from a programming language where whitespace doesn't matter.

Instruction:

Don't worry about understanding the code shown in the Figure below; just hit "Submit" to see what happens.

You should see an error message due to badly formatted code. We'll fix it in the next exercise!

```
script.py

1  def spam()
2    eggs = 12
3    return eggs
4
5  print spam()
```

Whitespace Means Right Space

Notice the error you got when you ran the code in the editor:

```
IndentationError: expected an indented block
```

You'll get this error whenever your Python whitespace is out of whack. (If you've studied JavaScript, think of improper whitespace as improper use of ; or { }.) When your punctuation's off, your meaning can change entirely:

The peasant said, "The witch turned me into a newt!"

"The peasant," said the witch, "turned me into a newt!"

See what we mean?

Instruction:

Properly indent the code to the right by hitting the spacebar key on your keyboard four times online 2 (before eggs) and another four times on line 3 (before return). Click "Save & Submit" once you've done this.

You should ALWAYS use 4 spaces to indent your code. See Figure below:

```
script.py

1  def spam():
2      eggs = 12
3      return eggs
4
5  print spam()
```

A Matter of Interpretation

In the introduction to this unit, we mentioned that Python is an **interpreted** language (meaning it runs using an **interpreter**). In the context, the interpreter is the console/output window in the top right corner of the page.

For now, think of the interpreter as a program that takes the code you write, checks it for syntax errors, and executes the statements in that code, line by line. It works as a go-between for you and the computer and lets you know the result of your instructions to the machine.

Instruction:

Tell Python to assign the value True to the variable spam and False to the variable eggs. See Figure below:

Single Line Comments

You may have noticed the instructions in the editor that begin with a # (**pound** or **hash**) symbol. These lines of code are called **comments**, and they aren't read by the interpreter— they don't affect the code at all. They're plain English comments written by the programmer to provide instructions or explain how a particular part of the program works.

Since this improves the readability of your code tremendously (and will help you debug programs more quickly, since you'll be able to tell at a glance what each part of the program is supposed to do), **we encourage you to comment on your code whenever its purpose isn't immediately obvious.**

Instruction:

Write a comment on line 1 in the editor. Make sure it starts with #! (It can say anything you like.) See Figure below:

```
script.py

1  #i love u
2
3  mysterious_variable = 42
```

Multi-Line Comments

Sometimes you have to write a *really* long comment. # will only work across a single line, and while you *could* write a multi-line comment and start each line with #, that can be a pain.

If you want to write a comment across multiple lines, you can include the whole block in a set of triple quotation marks, like so:

```
"""I'm a lumberjack and I'm okay
I sleep all night and I work all day!"""
```

Instruction:

Write a multi-line comment in the editor. Include whatever text you want! See Figure below:

```
script.py
1  """I am going to leave my job for the sake of my career in research and academia that could be of more
   use for my futurre achievements"""
```

Arithmetic Operators

Python's statements aren't limited to simple expressions of assignment like `spam = 3`; they can also include mathematical expressions using **arithmetic operators**.

There are six arithmetic operators we're going to focus on:

1. Addition (`+`)
2. Subtraction (`-`)
3. Multiplication (`*`)
4. Division (`/`)
5. Exponentiation (`**`)
6. Modulo (`%`)

Instruction:

Let's start with addition. Set the variable count_to to the sum of 1 + 2. See Figure below:

```
script.py

1   # Set count_to equal to 1 plus 2 on line 3!
2   count_to=1+2
3
4
5   print count_to
```

Subtraction

Good! Now let's try subtraction.

Instruction:

We've clearly counted too far with our count_to—we've gotten to five but want count_to to be smaller. Tell Python to reassign count_to to 5 - 2. See Figure below:

```
script.py
1  count_to = 5-2
2  """Four shalt thou not count, neither count thou two,
3  excepting that thou then proceed to three. Five is right out.
4  Change count_to to 5 minus 2!"""
5
6
7
8  print count_to
```

Multiplication

Perfect! Now let's try a little multiplication.

Instruction:

The Knights Who Say "Ni!" have only said "Ni!" twice. Let's make it twenty times by multiplying 2 * 10. See Figure below:

```
script.py
1  # Set ni to 2 times 10 on line 3!
2
3  ni = 2*10
4
5  print ni
```

Division

On second thought, 20 "Ni!"s might be a bit much. Let's use division to get it down to 5.

Instruction:

Set the value of ni to 5 (that is, 20 / 4). See Figure below:

```
script.py

1   # Set ni to 20 divided by 4 on line 3!
2
3   ni = 20/4
4
5   print ni
```

Exponentiation

Excellent job!

All the arithmetic operations you've done so far have probably either been intuitive or have resembled work you've done in other programming languages (such as JavaScript).**Exponentiation**, however, might be a new one, so it bears some explaining.

The `**` operator raises the first number, the **base**, to the power of the second number, the **exponent**. So if you type `2 **3`, you get `8` (`2 ** 3` is the same as `2 * 2 * 2`, both of which equal `8`). `5 ** 2 = 25`, `2 ** 4 = 16`, and so on.

Instruction:

Our lumberjack is super hungry and wants 100 eggs. Set eggs to 100 using exponentiation. See Figure below:

```
script.py

1  #Set eggs equal to 100 using exponentiation on line 3!
2
3  eggs =5**2*4
4
5  print eggs
```

Modulo

Impressive! That was a lot of eggs. Hope you left room for spam!

Our final arithmetic operator is **modulo** (also called **modulus**). Modulo returns the remainder left over by integer division. So, if you ask the Python interpreter to evaluate 5 % 2, it will return 1 (since 2 goes into 5 evenly two times, with 1 left over). 10 % 5 is 0, 113 % 100 is 13, and so on.

Instruction:

Turns out you did leave room for spam—but not much! Set spam equal to 1 using modulo. You can use any two numbers that will leave a remainder of 1 to do this. See Figure below:

```
script.py

1  #Set spam equal to 1 using modulo on line 3!
2
3  spam =5%2
4
5  print spam
```

Bringing It All Together

Nice work! So far you've learned about the following in Python:

• **Variables**, which are ways to store values for later use;

• **Data types** (such as **integers**, **floats**, and **booleans**);

• **Whitespace** (and why it's significant!);

• **Statements** (and how Python statements are like statements in regular English);

• **Comments** (and why they're good for your code!); and

• **Arithmetic operations** (including +, −, *, /, **, and %).

Instruction:

Let's put all our knowledge to work.

1. Write a single-line comment on line 1. It can be anything! (Make sure it starts with #!)
2. Declare a variable, monty, and set it equal to True.
3. Declare another variable, python, and set it equal to1.234.
4. Declare a third variable, monty_python, and set it equal to python squared.

See Figure below:

```
script.py

1   #I am goign to leave for switzerland
2   monty=True
3   python=1.234
4   monty_python=python**2
```

DAY-2

TIP CALCULATOR

Your Favorite Meal

This project is designed to complement Unit 1: Python Syntax. It assumes familiarity with *only* the material covered in that course.

You've just feasted on a truly delicious meal of Spam and eggs. The diner's computer is down, however, so you'll need to compute the cost of your meal yourself.

Here's how it'll break down:

Cost of meal: $44.50

Restaurant tax: 6.75%

Tip: 15%

You'll want to apply the tip to the overall cost of the meal (including tax).

Instruction:

First, let's declare a variable meal and assign it the value44.50. See Figure below:

```
script.py

1  # Assign the variable meal the value 44.50 on line 3!
2  meal=44.50
3
```

The Tax

Good! Now let's create a variable for the tax percentage.

The tax on your meal at this diner is 6.75%. Because we'll be multiplying with floats and not percentages, however, you'll have to divide 6.75 by 100 in order to get the decimal form of the number.

Instruction:

Create the variable tax and set it equal to the decimal value of 6.75%. See Figure below:

```
script.py
1  meal = 44.50
2  tax=6.75/100
```

The Tip

Nice work! You received good service at this diner, so you'd like to leave a 15% tip on top the cost of the meal (including tax).

Before we compute the tip for your overall bill, let's set a variable for the tip (15%). Again, this is a percentage, so you'll need to divide 15.0 by 100 in order to get the decimal form of the tip.

Instruction:

Set the variable tip to 15% (in decimal form!) on line 5. (You can just type 0.15 directly, if you like.) See the Figure below:

```
script.py

1   # You're almost there! Assign the tip variable on line 5.
2
3   meal = 44.50
4   tax = 0.0675
5   tip=15.0/100
```

Reassign in a Single Line

Okay! We've got the three variables we need to perform our calculation, and we know a bunch of arithmetic operators that will be able to help us out.

We saw in Lesson 1 that we could **reassign** a variable when needed—for example, we could say spam = 7 at one point in the program, then later change our minds and say spam = 3.

Instruction:

On line 7 in the editor, reassign meal to the value of itself + itself * tax (this will add the dollar amount of the tax to the cost of the meal). You're completely allowed to reassign a variable in terms of itself!

We're only calculating the cost of meal and tax here—we'll get to the tip soon!

See Figure below:

```
script.py

1   # Reassign meal on line 7!
2
3   meal = 44.50
4   tax = 0.0675
5   tip = 0.15
6
7   meal=44.50+44.50*0.0675
```

23

Second Verse, Same as the First

Well, *almost* the same. Here, we're going to introduce a new variable instead of resetting an existing variable.

Now that `meal`'s got the cost of the food + tax, let's introduce a new variable on line 8, `total`, that's equal to the new `meal` +`meal` * `tip`. (This should be very similar to what you just did in the last exercise.)

The code on line 10 will nicely format the value of `total` and will ensure it prints to the **console** with two numbers after the decimal. (We'll learn all about string formatting, the console, and the print keyword in Unit 2!)

Instruction:

Assign the variable total to the sum of meal + meal * tip on line 8, then hit "run" to see the total cost of your meal! See Figure below:

```
script.py

1   # Assign the variable total on line 8!
2
3   meal = 44.50
4   tax = 0.0675
5   tip = 0.15
6
7   meal = meal + meal * tax
8   total=meal+meal*tip
9
10  print("%.2f" % total)
```

DAY-3

STRINGS & CONSOLE OUTPUT

Step One: Strings

(This course assumes familiarity with the material presented in Lesson 1: Python Syntax.)

Another useful data type in Python is the **string**. Strings are, well, *strings* of characters, which is a more formal way of saying they're really just regular English phrases. They can include numbers, letters, and various symbols, like so: `"We're #1!"`

A **string literal** is a string created by *literally* just writing it down between quotation marks (`'` or `"`). You have to use the same type of quotation mark on each end of the string, though—no `'string"`s or `"string'`s!

Instruction:

Assign the string "Always look on the bright side of life!"to the variable brian.

See Figure given below:

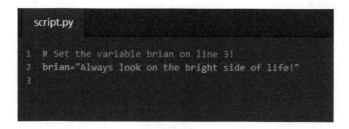

```
script.py
1  # Set the variable brian on line 3!
2  brian="Always look on the bright side of life!"
3
```

Step Two: Things

Excellent! Let's get a little practice in with strings. Set the following variables to the following phrases:

Instruction:

1. Set caesar to "Graham"
2. Set praline to "John"
3. Set viking to "Teresa"

See Figure given below:

```
script.py

1   # Assign your variables below, each on its own line!
2   caesar="Graham"
3   praline="John"
4   viking="Teresa"
5
6
7   # Put your variables above this line
8
9   print caesar
10  print praline
11  print viking
```

Step Three: Escape!

Don't get too comfortable: you can't use just *any* symbol in a string, and some results can only be achieved by special characters. The practice of including these characters in a string requires that these strings be **escaped**, or marked as unique. The backslash character (\) does this work for us! We just put it directly before the character we want to escape.

Instruction:

The string in the editor is broken: the apostrophe in I'm makes Python think the single-quote string ends there. Fix it by escaping the ' in I'm!

See Figure below:

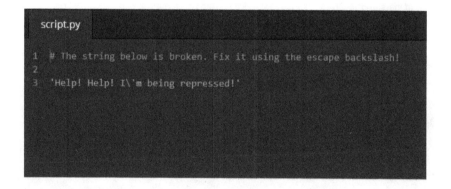

```
script.py

1   # The string below is broken. Fix it using the escape backslash!
2
3   'Help! Help! I\'m being repressed!'
```

Access by Offset

Great work! (By the way, you could also have repaired the string by replacing the single quotes on the ends with double quotes, like this: `"Help! Help! I'm being repressed!"`.)

Remember how we told you that strings were, technically speaking, strings of characters? Wouldn't it be nifty if you could get to each character in a string individually?

Well, you can!

Each character in a string has a **subscript** or **offset**, which is a fancy way of saying it has a number attached to it. The number starts at 0 for the leftmost character and increases by one as you move character-by-character to the right. Check out the diagram in the editor!

Instruction:

When you think you've got the hang of the code in the editor, set fifth_letter equal to the fifth letter of the string "MONTY", like so: "MONTY"[?] (but replace the ? with the correct number).

See Figure below:

```
script.py

1   """
2   The string "PYTHON" has six characters,
3   numbered 0 to 5, as shown below:
4
5   +---+---+---+---+---+---+
6   | P | Y | T | H | O | N |
7   +---+---+---+---+---+---+
8     0   1   2   3   4   5
9
10  So if you wanted "Y", you could just type
11  "PYTHON"[1] (always start counting from 0!)
12  """
13  fifth_letter = "MONTY"[4]
14
15  print fifth_letter
```

Four Methods to the Madness

Great work! Now we're going to talk about some of the **methods** that are available for use with strings.

We'll explain methods much more in future lessons, but for now, the takeaway is that string methods are pre-built pieces of code that perform specific tasks for strings.

We're going to focus on four string methods in this section:

1. `len()`
2. `lower()`
3. `upper()`
4. `str()`

Let's start with `len()`, which gets the length of a string!

Instruction:

On line 1, create a variable called parrot and set it to the string "Norwegian Blue" (be sure to include the space and capitalize exactly as shown!).

Then, on line 2, type len (parrot) after the word print, like so: print len (parrot). This will print out the number of letters in "Norwegian Blue"!

See Figure below:

```
script.py
1  parrot="Norwegian Blue"
2  print len (parrot)
```

lower()

Well done! Again, `len()` returns the length—that is, the number of characters—of the string on which it's called.

Let's say that you don't want any capitalization in your string, though (in this case, `"Norwegian Blue"`). In this example, it's a tiny amount of work to manually change `"Norwegian Blue"` to "30orwegian blue". But what if you wanted to convert thousands of words to all-lower case? Doing it manually would take forever.

Instruction:

Python is all about automation! Call lower() on parrot (after the word print) on line 3 in the editor, like so: parrot.lower(). This will make the string all lower-case! (This is different from the way you call len(), and we'll explain the reasoning behind this before this section is over.)

See Figure below:

```
script.py

1   parrot = "Norwegian Blue"
2
3   print parrot.lower()
```

upper()

Perfect! Now your string is 100% lower case.

Instruction:

Unfortunately, you just realized you actually need your string to be completely upper case, not lower. Call upper() on parrot(after the word print on line 3) in order to fix this in one fell swoop!

See Figure below:

```
script.py
1  parrot = "norwegian blue"
2
3  print parrot.upper()
```

str()

It looks like you're really getting the hang of string methods in Python. In case you're getting a bit bored (and we know adjusting string capitalization isn't the most exciting thing in the world), try the `str()` method on for size!

The `str()` method returns a string containing a nicely printable representation of whatever you put between the parentheses. It makes strings out of non-strings! For example,

```
str(2)
```

would turn 2 into "2".

Instruction:

Two steps here:

1. Create a variable pi and set it to 3.14 on line 4.
2. Call str (pi) on line 5, after the print keyword.

See Figure below:

```
script.py

1  """Declare and assign your variable on line 4,
2  then call your method on line 5!"""
3
4  pi=3.14
5  print str (pi)
```

Dot Notation

As promised, we'll now explain the reason you use `len(string)` and `str(object)`, but **dot notation**(*e.g.* `"String".upper()`) for the rest.

Dot notation works on string literals (`"The Ministry of Silly Walks".upper()`) and variables assigned to strings (`ministry.upper()`) because these methods are specific to strings—that is, they don't work on anything else.

By contrast, `len()` and `str()` can work on a whole bunch of different objects (which we'll get to later), so they aren't tied to strings with dot notation.

Instruction:

Let's do just a bit more practice. Call len() on ministry on line 3 and upper() on line 4 (do this after the print keyword each time).

See Figure below:

```
script.py

1  ministry = "The Ministry of Silly Walks"
2
3  print len(ministry)
4  print ministry.upper()
```

Printing with String Literals

The area to the right of these instructions is the **editor**, which is where we've been writing our code.

Python translates your instructions to instructions the computer can understand with an **interpreter**. You can think of the interpreter as a little program that ferries information between your Python code and the computer when you click "Save & Submit Code." The actual window to which the interpreter spits out the output of your code is the **console** (the window in the upper right).

If you're familiar with JavaScript, then you know that `console.log` **logs** the result of evaluating your code to the console; `print` is Python's version of `console.log`.

If you haven't studied JavaScript, never fear! All you need to know is that `print` *prints* the result of the interpreter's evaluation of your code to the console for you to see.

Instruction:

Let's start with something simple. Try `print`ing `"Monty Python"` to the console. The syntax looks like this:

```
print "Your string goes here"
```

Don't forget the quotes (' or")!

See Figure below:

```
script.py

1  """Tell Python to print "Monty Python"
2  to the console on line 4!"""
3  print "Monty Python"
4
```

Printing with Variables

Great! Now let's combine what we've learned about variables with our new `print` keyword.

Instruction:

1. Declare a variable called the_machine_goes and assign it the string value "Ping!" on line 5. Make sure to type "Ping!"exactly as shown—complete with capital "P" and an exclamation point!
2. Go ahead and printthe_machine_goes on line 6.

See Figure below:

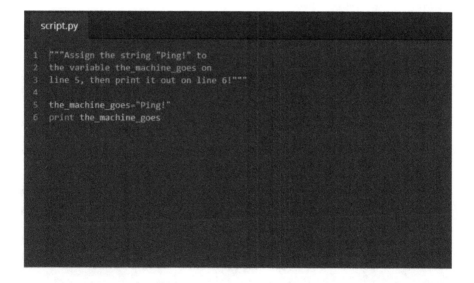

```
script.py
1  """Assign the string "Ping!" to
2  the variable the_machine_goes on
3  line 5, then print it out on line 6!"""
4
5  the_machine_goes="Ping!"
6  print the_machine_goes
```

String Concatenation

You know about strings, and you know about arithmetic operators. But did you know some arithmetic operators work on strings?

If you use the + operator between two strings, it **concatenates** them (glues them together).

print "Monty " + "Python"

will print out "Monty Python"!

Instruction:

Give it a go in the editor. Print the concatenated strings "Spam ", "and ", "eggs" on line 3 to print the string "Spam and eggs" to the console.

See Figure below:

```
script.py

1    # Print the concatenation of "Spam and eggs" on line 3!
2
3    print "Spam" + " and " "eggs"
```

Explicit String Conversion

Remember when we talked about the `str()` method a couple of lessons back, and how it turns non-strings into strings? The fancy name for that process is **explicit string conversion**.

You're *explicitly* telling Python, "Hey, I know this isn't a string, but I want to turn it into one." Contrast this with just putting quotes around a sequence of characters to make it a string.

Making a number into a string can let you glue together strings and numbers (which Python normally won't allow). Check it out:

```python
print "I have " + str(2) + " coconuts!"
```

will print `"I have 2 coconuts!"`

Instruction:

1. Run the code as-is. You get an error!
2. Use str() to turn 3.14 into a string, then run the code again.

See Figure below:

```
script.py

1   # Turn 3.14 into a string on line 3!
2
3   print "The value of pi is around " + str(3.14)
```

String Formatting with %, Part 1

Awesome work so far. This is the last new thing to cover before we review!

We saw earlier that you can access individual characters in a string by **offset**, or, if you want to think about it this way, ID number. (Remember, `"PYTHON"[1]` is `"Y"`, not `"P"`!)

Unfortunately, strings in Python are **immutable**—you can't change them once they're created.

However, there *is* a way you can work flexibility into your strings, and that's with **string formatting**. It uses the %symbol (don't confuse this with modulo!), and you can sort of think of it as a variable for your string.

Instruction:

Take a look at the code in the editor. What do you think it'll do? Click Save & Submit Code when you think you know.

See Figure below:

```
script.py

1   string_1 = "Camelot"
2   string_2 = "place"
3
4   print "Let's not go to %s. 'Tis a silly %s." % (string_1, string_2)
```

String Formatting with %, Part 2

Did you see that? The `%` string formatter replaced the `%s` (the "s" is for "string") in our string with the variables in parentheses. (We could have done that by just putting `"Camelot"` and `"place"` in parentheses after the string, but we wanted to show you how it works with variables.)

The syntax went like this:

```
print "%s" % (string_variable)
```

You can have as many variables (or strings!) separated by commas between your parentheses as you like:

```
print "The %s who %s %s!" % ("Knights", "say", "Ni")
```

prints `"The Knights who say Ni!"`

Instruction:

For our grand finale, we're showing you a bit of new code. Don't worry if you don't get how it works yet; we'll explain it soon!

For now, replace the ___s with the form of % you need to complete your quest: %s inside the string, and % to link the string with its arguments.

See Figure below (before replacement):

```
script.py
1  name = raw_input("What is your name?")
2  quest = raw_input("What is your quest?")
3  color = raw_input("What is your favorite color?")
4
5  print "Ah, so your name is ___, your quest is ___, " \
6  "and your favorite color is ___." ___ (name, quest, color)
```

See Figure below (after replacement):

```
script.py

1  name = "adeel"
2  quest = "css"
3  color = "pink"
4
5  print "Ah, so your name is %s, your quest is %s, " \
6  "and your favorite color is %s." % (name, quest, color)
```

It will print out like this:

```
Ah, so your name is adeel, your quest is css, and your favorite color is pink.
None
```

And Now, For Something Completely Familiar

Great job! You've learned a lot in this unit, including:

- What strings are, and how to create them literally (using ' ' or " ") or explicitly (using the `str()` method);
- string methods, such as `len()`, `upper()`, and `lower()`;
- the `print` keyword for outputting Python's evaluation of your code to the console; and
- advanced printing techniques using %.

Let's wrap it all up!

Instruction:

1. Create a variable called my_string and set it to any string you'd like.
2. Go ahead and print its len()gth on line 4.
3. Go for the gold and print its.upper() case version on line 5.

See Figure below:

```
script.py

1  # Write your code below, starting on line 3!
2
3  my_string="adeel"
4  print len("adeel")
5  print "adeel".upper()
```

It will print out length of words and words in Upper case like this:

```
5
ADEEL
None
```

41

DAY-4

DATE AND TIME

The datetime Library

In this small project, we'll create a program that experiments with Python's ability to give us the current date and time. This will give you some practice with printing strings, concatenation, and the `str()` explicit conversion function.

At the end of this section, you'll know how to print the date and time in the following format: mm/dd/yyyy hh:mm:ss.

On line 1, notice the statement `from datetime import datetime`. Importing special functionality into your programs will be covered in Unit 4's discussion of the import statement.

For now, just know that we're telling the Python interpreter to give our program the ability to retrieve the current date and time.

In the next exercise, we'll cover how to explicitly retrieve this information!

Instruction:

The datetime import code goes as shown in Figure below:

```
script.py
1  from datetime import datetime
2
3
```

Getting the Current Date and Time

To retrieve the current date and time, we can use a function called `datetime.now()` to get that information.

In a later course, you'll learn all about **functions**. For now, just know that `datetime.now()` calls on a piece of code that comes with Python that figures out the current date and time for us.

Instruction:

1. Create a variable called now and store the result of datetime.now() in it. We'll use this variable in the next exercise.
2. Go ahead and print the value of the variable now.

See Figure below:

```
script.py
1  from datetime import datetime
2  now=datetime.now()
3  print now
```

It will return Date and Time as shown in Figure below:

```
2013-11-09 16:53:00.219915
None
```

Extracting Information

Notice how we got an output of the form `2012-07-19 12:50:53`.180759. That's pretty ugly.

Let's examine how to extract portions of the date and time to eventually print out a "prettier" form of this information.

Let's start by retrieving the month, day, and year from the result of `datetime.now()`. To do this, we can use our variable `now` in the following way: `current_year` = now.year.

Of course, the variable on the left-hand side of the assignment could be named anything.

The fact that we can extract parts of the date in such an elegant syntax is pretty awesome. As you could guess, we can use a similar syntax to extract the `month` and `day`.

Note: Don't worry about the details of the notation `now.year`. It's called **dot notation** and it's used to access data from an **object.** We mentioned this briefly in Unit 2and will talk much more about objects later.

Instruction:

Go ahead and print out the current month, day, and year to the console on separate lines.

See Figure below:

```
script.py

1   from datetime import datetime
2   current_month=now.month
3   current_day=now.day
4   current_year=now.year
5   print current_month, current_day, current_year
```

It will return the values as shown below:

```
11 9 2013
None
```

Hot Date

Great job printing out the date's components! In gearing up for our ultimate goal of printing out `mm/dd/yyyy hh:mm:ss`, let's tackle adding `/` slashes to the date's parts.

You might think to do something like:

```
print now.month, "/", now.day, "/", now.year
```

However, **this would incorrectly give you spaces between the slashes.** Hence, the better solution is to use string concatenation (the +operator), covered in Unit 2.
As you'll see, it's not as simple as just using concatenation—mainly because *concatenation only works with strings*.

When you extract information like `now.year`, you end up with an integer (a positive or negative whole number). To convert an integer to a string, you can use the `str()` function. For example, if a variable `x` had the value `4` and we wanted to convert that into `"4"`, you could type:

```
str(x)
```

Instruction:

Print out the current date in the pretty form of mm/dd/yyyy. It's totally okay if it comes out as m/d/yyyy.

See Figure below:

```
script.py
1  from datetime import datetime
2  current_month=now.month
3  current_day=now.day
4  current_year=now.year
5  print str(now.month) +"/"+str(now.day) +"/"+str(now.year)
```

It will return values as shown below:

```
11/9/2013
None
```

Pretty Time

Nice work! Let's do the same for the parts of the time—namely, the hour, minute, and second.

As you might guess, we can also use our variable `now` to print out the time information. If you wanted to print out the current hour, you could do:

```
current_hour = now.hour
```

Just for clarification, our variable `now` contains the results of `datetime.now()`; there's nothing special about naming the variable "now." It's just for convenience!

Instruction:

Similar to the last exercise, print out the current time in the pretty form of hh:mm:ss. Remember to use string concatenation.

Note: It's also okay if you end up with h:m:s.

See Figure below:

```
script.py
1   from datetime import datetime
2   current_hour= now.hour
3   current_minute= now.minute
4   current_second= now.second
5   print str(now.hour)+ ":"+ str(now.minute)+ ":"+ str(now.second)
```

It will return values like this:

```
16:53:0
None
```

Grand Finale

So far, we've managed to prettily print the date and time separately. Let's combine the two!

Instruction:

Print out the date and time together in the form: mm/dd/yyyy hh:mm:ss

(Note that a space separates the date and time, so you'll need the + operator once more.)

See Figure below:

```
script.py
1  from datetime import datetime
2  current_month= now.month
3  current_day= now.day
4  current_year= now.year
5  current_hour=now.hour
6  current_minute=now.minute
7  current_second=now.second
8  print str(now.month)+ "/"+ str(now.day)+ "/"+ str(now.year), str(now.hour)+ ":"+ str(now.minute)+ ":"+
   str(now.second)
```

It will return values like this:

```
11/9/2013 16:53:0
None
```

DAY-5

CONDITIONALS AND CONTROL FLOW

Go With the Flow

(This course assumes familiarity with the material presented in Unit 1: Python Syntax and Unit 2: Strings & Console Output. From here on out, take for granted that each new course assumes knowledge of the material presented in the previous courses.)

You may have noticed that the Python programs we've been writing so far have had sort of one-track minds. They compute the sum of two numbers or `print` something to the console, but they don't have the ability to pick one outcome over another—say, add two numbers if their sum is less than 100, or instead `print` the numbers to the console without adding them if their sum is greater than 100.

Control flow allows us to have these multiple outcomes and to select one based on what's going on in the program. Different outcomes can be produced based on user input or any number of factors in the program's **environment**. (The environment is the technical name for all the variables—and their values—that exist in the program at a given time.)

Instruction:

Check out the code in the editor. To help keep you motivated, we've provided a glimpse into the not-so-distant future: the type of program you'll be able to write once you've mastered control flow. Write this Code to see what happens!

See Figure below:

```
script.py

1 - def clinic():
2       print "You've just entered the clinic!"
3       print "Do you take the door on the left or the right?"
4       answer = raw_input("Type left or right and hit 'Enter'.").lower()
5 -     if answer == "left" or answer == "l":
6           print "This is the Verbal Abuse Room, you heap of parrot droppings!"
7 -     elif answer == "right" or answer == "r":
8           print "Of course this is the Argument Room, I've told you that already!"
9 -     else:
10          print "You didn't pick left or right! Try again."
11          clinic()
12
13  clinic()
```

It will return values like this:

```
You've just entered the clinic!
Do you take the door on the left or the right?
Type left or right and hit 'Enter'. left
This is the Verbal Abuse Room, you heap of parrot droppings!
None
```

Note: Type left or right and hit "Enter" when prompted.

Compare Closely!

Let's not get ahead of ourselves. First, we'll start with the simplest aspect of control flow: **comparators**. There are six of them, and we're willing to bet at least a few look familiar:

1. Equal to (==)
2. Not equal to (!=)
3. Less than (<)
4. Less than or equal to (<=)
5. Greater than (>)
6. Greater than or equal to (>=)

Note that == is used to compare whether two things are equal, and = is used to assign a value to a variable.

We hope you're familiar with the ideas of greater/less than and greater/less than or equal to (though you've probably seen the latter written like this: ≥ and ≤). They work exactly as you think they would: they test to see if a number is (or is not) equal to, greater than (or equal to), or less than (or equal to) another number.

(If you're coming from the JavaScript track: there is no ===in Python.)

Instruction:

Let's run through the comparators in the editor. Set each variable to either True or False depending on what you think the result will be. For example, 1 < 2 will be True, because one is less than two.

1. Set bool_one equal to the result of 17 < 118 % 100
2. Set bool_two equal to the result of 100 == 33 * 3 + 1
3. Set bool_three equal to the result of 19 <= 2**4
4. Set bool_four equal to the result of -22 >= -18
5. Set bool_five equal to the result of 99 != 98 + 1

See Figure below:

```
script.py
1   # Assign True or False as appropriate on the lines below!
2   bool_one = 17<118%100
3
4   bool_two = 100==33*3+1
5
6   bool_three = 19<=2**4
7
8   bool_four = -22>=-18
9
10  bool_five = 99!=98+1
```

Compare... Closelier

Excellent! It looks like you're comfortable with basic expressions and comparators.

But what about... *extreme* expressions and comparators?

(This exercise may seem unnecessary to you, but we can't tell you the number of problems caused in programs by incorrect order of operations or reversed >s and <s. Bugs like this can be a serious problem!)

Instruction:

Let's run through the comparators in the editor one more time (these expressions are more complex than what you saw in the last exercise). Again, set each variable to either True or False depending on what you think the result of the evaluation will be.

1. Set bool_one to the result of20 + -10 * 2 > 10 % 3 % 2
2. Set bool_two to the result of(10 + 17)**2 == 3**6
3. Set bool_three to the result of 1**2**3 <= -(-(-1))
4. Set bool_four to the result of40 / 20 * 4 >= -4**2
5. Set bool_five to the result of100**0.5 != 6 + 4

See Figure below:

```
script.py

1    # Assign True or False as appropriate on the lines below!
2
3    bool_one = False
4
5    bool_two = True
6
7    bool_three = False
8
9    bool_four = True
10
11   bool_five = False
```

How the Tables Have Turned

Nice work!

Based on our comparisons, you've probably guessed that comparisons in Python generate one of two results: True or False. These are instances of a data type we mentioned briefly in Unit 1 called **booleans**, and they are the *only* two instances. Things aren't "sort of True" or "Falseish" or "maybe" in Python—they are True or False (and are always capitalized, unlike in JavaScript).

Let's reverse things a bit: we'll supply the boolean value (True or False), and you write an expression that evaluates appropriately.

Instruction:

For each boolean value in the editor, write an expression that evaluates to that value. Feel free to write expressions that are as simple or as complex as you'd like! Remember, though: simple is better than complex!

Remember, comparators are: ==, !=, >, >=, <, and <=. Make sure to use at least three different ones. And don't just use True and False! That's cheating!

See Figure below:

```
script.py
1  # Create comparative statements as appropriate on the lines below!
2
3  # Make me true!
4  bool_one = 4==2*2
5
6  # Make me false!
7  bool_two = 10<3*4%2
8
9  # Make me true!
10 bool_three = 9!=2**2+1
11
12 # Make me false!
13 bool_four = 2>=4*2+1
14
15 # Make me true!
16 bool_five = 6<=4*3**2
```

To Be and/or Not to Be

Boolean operators (or **logical operators**) are words used to connect Python statements in a grammatically correct way—almost exactly as in regular English. There are three boolean operators in Python:

1. and, which means the same as it does in English;

2. or, which means "one or the other OR BOTH" (it's not *exclusively* one or the other, the way it often is in English);

3. not, which means the same as it does in English.

We want to stress this second case to you: if your mom tells you that you can have *Monty Python and the Holy Grail* **or** *Monty Python's Life of Brian*, she probably means "one or the other, but not both." Python, on the other hand, would be totally fine with your picking both, so long as you don't pick *neither*. Python is cooler than your mom.

Boolean operators result (predictably) in boolean values—`True` or `False`. We'll go through the three operators one by one.

Instruction:

Before we get started with and, take a look at the truth table in the editor. (This is for those of you who like to see the bigger picture before we dive into the details.) Don't worry if you don't completely get it yet—you will by the end of this section!

See Figure below:

```
script.py

1    """
2        Boolean Operators
3    ----------------------------
4    True and True is True
5    True and False is False
6    False and True is False
7    False and False is False
8
9    True or True is True
10   True or False is True
11   False or True is True
12   False or False is False
13
14   Not True is False
15   Not False is True
16
17   """
```

And

The boolean operator `and` only results in `True` when the **expressions** on either side of `and` are *both* true. An expression is any statement involving one or more variables and operators (arithmetic, logical, or boolean). For instance:

`1 < 2 and 2 < 3` results in `True` because it is true that one is less than two **and** that two is less than three.

`1 < 2 and 2 > 3` results in `False` because it is **not true** that both statements are true—one is less than two, but two is **not** greater than three.

Instruction:

Let's practice a bit with and. Assign the boolean values beneath each expression as appropriate. This may seem overkill, but remember: practice makes perfect.

1. Set bool_one equal to the result of False and False
2. Set bool_two equal to the result of -(-(-(-2))) == -2and 4 >= 16**0.5
3. Set bool_three equal to the result of 19 % 4 != 300 / 10 /10 and False
4. Set bool_four equal to the result of -(1**2) < 2**0 and10 % 10 <= 20 - 10 * 2
5. Set bool_five equal to the result of True and True

See Figure below:

```
script.py

1   bool_one = 2<3 and 3>4
2
3   bool_two = False and True
4
5   bool_three = False and False
6
7   bool_four = -(1**2)<2**0 and 10%10 <=20-10*2
8
9   bool_five = 6==3*2 and 10>=2**2
```

Or

The boolean operator `or` only returns `True` when *either* (meaning one, the other *or both!*) of the expressions on each side of `or` are true. (It's only `False` when *both* expressions are `False`.) For example:

- `1 < 2 or 2 > 3` is `True`, even though two is not greater than three;
- `1 > 2 or 2 > 3` is `False`, because it is neither the case that one is greater than two nor that two is greater than three.

Instruction:

Time to practice with or!

1. Set bool_one equal to the result of 2**3 == 108 % 100 or 'Cleese' == 'King Arthur'
2. Set bool_two equal to the result of True or False
3. Set bool_three equal to the result of 100**0.5 >= 50 or False
4. Set bool_four equal to the result of True or True
5. Set bool_five equal to the result of 1**100 == 100**1 or3 * 2 * 1 != 3 + 2 + 1

See Figure below:

```
script.py

1  bool_one = True
2
3  bool_two = 2>1 or 4==2**3
4
5  bool_three = False
6
7  bool_four = 4==2*2 or 2**3==8
8
9  bool_five = False
```

Not

The boolean operator `not` returns `True` for false statements and `False` for true statements. Remember, the only two boolean values are `True` and `False`!

For example:

`not False` will evaluate to `True`, as will `not 40 > 41`. Applying `not` to expressions that would otherwise be true makes them `False`.

Instruction:

Last but not least, let's get some practice in with not.

1. Set bool_one equal to the result of not True
2. Set bool_two equal to the result of not 3**4 < 4**3
3. Set bool_three equal to the result of not 10 % 3 <= 10 % 2
4. Set bool_four equal to the result of not 3**2 + 4**2 !=5**2
5. Set bool_five equal to the result of not not False

See Figure below:

```
script.py

1   bool_one = 1==2+1
2
3   bool_two = not False
4
5   bool_three = not False
6
7   bool_four = not False
8
9   bool_five = 1>3
```

This and That (or This, But Not That!)

Fun fact: boolean operators can be chained together!

It's important to know that boolean operators are not evaluated straight across from left to right all the time; just like with arithmetic operators, where / and * are evaluated before + and - (remember Please Excuse My Dear Aunt Sally?), there is an **order of precedence** or **order of operations** for boolean operators. The order is as follows:

1. `not` is evaluated first;
2. `and` is evaluated next;
3. `or` is evaluated last.

This order can be changed by including parentheses (`()`). Anything in parentheses is evaluated as its own unit.

For instance, `True or not False and False` returns `True`.

Best practice: always use parentheses (`()`) to group your expressions to ensure they're evaluated in the order you want. Remember: explicit is better than implicit!

Instruction:

Go ahead and assign True or False as appropriate for bool_one through bool_five. No math in this one!

1. Set bool_one equal to the result of False or not True and True
2. Set bool_two equal to the result of False and not True or True
3. Set bool_three equal to the result of True and not (False or False)
4. Set bool_four equal to the result of not not True or False and not True
5. Set bool_five equal to the result of False or not (True and True)

See Figure below:

```
script.py

1   bool_one = False
2
3   bool_two = True
4
5   bool_three = True
6
7   bool_four = True
8
9   bool_five = False
```

Mix 'n Match

Great work! We're almost done with boolean operators.

Instruction:

Finally, let's try it the other way 'round—we'll provide the expected result (True or False), and you use any combination of boolean operators you want to achieve that result.

Remember, the boolean operators are and, or, and not. Make sure to use at least one and, or, or not.

See Figure below:

```
1    # Use boolean expressions as appropriate on the lines below!
2
3    # Make me false!
4    bool_one = 1+2==2 and 3<=2
5
6    # Make me true!
7    bool_two = 3**2>10 or 3*2>=6
8
9    # Make me false!
10   bool_three = 2*2==6 and 2*2==6
11
12   # Make me true!
13   bool_four = 4*5<=50 and 50>=2*25
14
15   # Make me true!
16   bool_five = 2**3!=6 or 3*2==6
```

Conditional Statement Syntax

Remember when we showed you that whitespace in Python is significant? If not, write this down: *whitespace in Python is significant*. If you've learned any JavaScript here, you know that the block of code an `if` statement executes is bound by curly braces (`{}`). In Python, whitespace (tabs or spaces) does this work for us.

Here's an example of `if` statement syntax in Python:

```
if 8 < 9:
    print "Eight is less than nine!"
```

`if` is always followed by an expression, which is followed by a colon (`:`). The **code block** (the code to be executed if the expression evaluates to `True`) is indented **four spaces**.

This is also true for `elif` and `else` (which we'll get to in a moment). The full syntax would look something like this:

```
if 8 < 9:
    print "I get printed!"
elif 8 > 9:
    print "I don't get printed."
else:
    print "I also don't get printed!"
```

Instruction:

Here's a piece of code that should look familiar: it's a snippet from the example we showed you in 1.1, "Introduction to Control Flow." If you think the print statement will print to the console, set response equal to 'Y'; otherwise, set response equal to 'N'. See Figure below:

```
script.py

1   response = 'Y'
2
3   answer = "Left"
4 - if answer == "Left":
5       print "This is the Verbal Abuse Room, you heap of parrot droppings!"
6
7   # Will the above print statement print to the console?
8   # Set response to 'Y' if you think so, and 'N' if you think not.
```

If You're Having...

Let's get some practice in with `if` statements. Remember, the syntax looks like this:

```
if EXPRESSION:
    # block line one
    # block line two
    # et cetera
```

Instruction:

In the editor you'll notice two functions. Don't worry about anything unfamiliar here. We'll explain it all in a few sections.

Your only job is to fill in the two if statements correctly. Make sure both expressions are True so that "Success #1" and "Success #2" are printed to the console.

See Figure below:

```
script.py

1  def using_control_once():
2      if 1<2:
3          return "Success #1"
4
5  def using_control_again():
6      if 3>1:
7          return "Success #2"
8
9  print using_control_once()
10 print using_control_again()
```

It will return values like this:

```
Success #1
Success #2
None
```

Else Problems, I Feel Bad for You, Son...

The `else` statement in Python is the complement to the `if` statement. While an `if` statement will return control of the program to the next line of code after the `if` code block even if there's no `else` statement, it's considered a good habit to pair each `if` with an `else`.

An `if`/`else` pair says to Python: "If this expression is true, run this indented code block; otherwise, run this code after the `else` statement."

Remember when we said "set `response` equal to `'Y'`, otherwise, set it to `'N'`" in the first exercise of this section? That was a kind of `if`/`else` statement!

`else` is always written alone. Unlike `if`, `else` should have nothing after it except a colon.

Instruction:

Complete the else statements. Remember to capitalize your booleans, and note the indentation for each line! It's important. See Figure below:

```
script.py
1   answer = "'Tis but a scratch!"
2
3   def black_knight():
4       if answer == "'Tis but a scratch!":
5           return True
6       else:
7           return        # Make sure this returns False
8
9   def french_soldier():
10      if answer == "Go away, or I shall taunt you a second time!":
11          return True
12      else:
13          return        # Make sure this returns False
```

To complete else statement you will just add "False" on Line 8 and Line 14 as shown in the Figure below:

```
script.py
1    answer = "'Tis but a scratch!"
2
3 ▾ def black_knight():
4 ▾     if answer == "'Tis but a scratch!":
5            return True
6 ▾     else:
7            return        # Make sure this returns False
8        False
9 ▾ def french_soldier():
10 ▾    if answer == "Go away, or I shall taunt you a second time!":
11           return True
12 ▾    else:
13           return        # Make sure this returns False
14       False
```

I Got 99 Problems, But a Switch Ain't One

"Elif" is short for "else if." It means exactly what it sounds like: "otherwise, if the following code is true, do this!"

If you're coming from JavaScript, you may know that you have two choices when you have a chain of conditional statements: a bunch of `else if` statements, or a `switch` statement. Python simplifies this for you: there's only `elif`.

Instruction:

1. On line 2, fill in the if statement to check if answer is greater than 5.
2. On line 4, fill in the elif so that the function outputs -1 if answer is less than 5.

See Figure below:

```
script.py
1   def greater_less_equal_5(answer):
2       if
3           return 1
4       elif
5           return -1
6       else:
7           return 0
8
9   print greater_less_equal_5(4)
10  print greater_less_equal_5(5)
11  print greater_less_equal_5(6)
12
```

The values will be set like this:

```
script.py
1   def greater_less_equal_5(answer):
2       if answer >5:
3           return 1
4       elif answer <5:
5           return -1
6       else:
7           return 0
8
9   print greater_less_equal_5(4)
10  print greater_less_equal_5(5)
11  print greater_less_equal_5(6)
12
```

It will return values like this:

```
-1
0
1
None
```

The Big If

Really great work! Here's what you've learned in this unit:

1. Basics of control flow;

2. Comparators (such as >, <, and ==);

3. Boolean operators (and, or, and not);

4. And conditional statements (if, else, and elif).

Let's get to the grand finale.

Instruction:

Write an if statement in the_flying_circus(). It must include:

1. and, or, or not;
2. ==, !=, <, <=, >, or >=;
3. an if, elif, AND else statement;
4. it must return True when evaluated.

See Figure below:

```
script.py

1   def the_flying_circus():
2       # Start coding here!
```

The code will go like this:

```
script.py

1   answer="Adeel"
2
3   def the_flying_circus():
4       if answer== "Adeel":
5           return True
6       elif answer== "Adeel and Rehan":
7           return False
8       else:
9           return False
```

DAY-6

PYG LATIN

Break It Down

When you start a big project like this, it's important to take some time to break the problem into individual steps. Then you can tackle (and test) one step at a time rather than trying to write a huge program all at once!

Let's think about the PygLatin problem. Pig Latin is a language where we take the first letter of a word and put it on the end while also adding a vowel sound. So dog becomes "ogday". What are the steps we need to take?

1. Ask the user to input a word in English
2. Check to make sure the user entered a valid word
3. Convert the word from English to Pig Latin
4. Display the translation result

Notice that some of the steps can themselves be broken down into individual steps. For example, we'll want to think through the algorithm for step #3 before we start coding.

A little bit of time invested in thinking through the decomposition of and algorithms for your program can save you a LOT of frustration down the road!

Get a piece of paper and work out an algorithm for step #3 of the project.

Since we took the time to write out the steps for our solution, you'll know what's coming next!

Ahoy! (or Should I Say Ahoyay!)

This project will be a workout, so let's warm up by printing a welcome message for our translator users.

Instruction:

Use Python to print "Welcome to the English to Pig Latin translator!" to the console.

See Figure below:

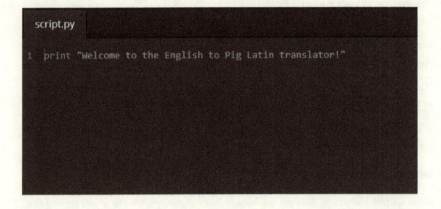

Input!

If we're going to translate an English word into Pig Latin, the first thing we're going to need is a word.

Python can ask for input from the user with the `raw_input` command. For example, if you type:

```
name = raw_input("What's your name?")
```

Python will print:

```
What's your name? >
```

Once you type something and hit Enter, Python will store whatever you typed in the `name` variable.

Instruction:

Below your existing code, prompt the user to enter a word, and store it in a variable called original. The prompt message can be whatever you want!

See Figure below:

```
script.py

1  print "Welcome to the English to Pig Latin translator!"
2  original= raw_input("What is your name")
```

Check Yourself!

Whenever you ask a user for input, it's a good idea to check the result that you get before you use it in your program.

In this case, we want to make sure that the input is something we can reliably translate into Pig Latin. That is, we want to make sure we got something resembling an English word.

The first thing we can check is that there are characters in our string. Let's check to make sure the string isn't empty. How can we check to make sure that our original variable isn't empty?

Instruction:

Write an if statement that checks to see if the string is not empty.

1. If the string is *not* empty, print the user's word.
2. Otherwise (else), print "empty" if the string is empty.

Make sure you thoroughly test your code. You'll want to make sure you run it multiple times and test both an empty string and a string with characters. When you are confident that your code works, continue on to the next exercise.

```
script.py

1    print "Welcome to the English to Pig Latin translator!"
2    original= raw_input("What is your name")
3 ▾  if len(original)>0:
4        print original
5 ▾  else:
6        print "empty"
```

Note: When you will enter the code it will prompt you to enter your name and when entered it will return the name as "original" as set out in print original. If you enter a value of "0" the code will return empty as set out in else: statement.

Check Yourself... Some More

Great! Now we know we have a non-empty string. Let's be even more thorough, though. After all, a user might try to be tricky and enter something like 8675309 which, since it is numbers not letters, would not make sense in PygLatin.

Let's add to our input validation and make sure that the word the user enters contains only alphabetical characters. You can use the `isalpha()` function to check this. To check if the string `"J123"` within a variable `x` is alphabetical, you could do:

```
x = "J123"
x.isalpha()  # False
```

Instruction:

Add onto your if condition to check that the word is also composed of all alphabetical characters. You should end up with a single if-else statement that makes sure original is a non-empty alphabetical string.

Make sure to check both an all-alphabetical string and one with letters and numbers!

The code should go like this:

```
script.py
1  print "Welcome to the English to Pig Latin translator!"
2  original= raw_input("What is your name")
3  if len(original)>0 and original.isalpha():
4      print original
5  else:
6      print "empty"
```

Note: With this code you will get "empty" when you will enter anything other than alphabets.

Pop Quiz!

Teachers sometimes give pop quizzes to make sure their students are mastering current material. Similarly, when you're working on a big project, you should periodically take time to really put your program to the test.

When you finish one part of your program, it's important to test it multiple times, using a variety of inputs.

Instruction:

Take some time right now to test your current code. Make sure you try some inputs that should pass the word test and some that should fail. Enter some strings that contain non-alphabetical characters and an empty string.

When you're convinced your code is ready to go, click Save & Submit Code to move on to the next step!

Look at code again:

```
script.py
1   print "Welcome to the English to Pig Latin translator!"
2   original= raw_input("What is your name")
3   if len(original)>0 and original.isalpha():
4       print original
5   else:
6       print "empty"
```

Test your code now by inputting different values. Enter different words and numerical values as well to check the authenticity of your code. Keep in mind that "code validation" is an integral part of programming process.

Ay B C

Now that we know we have a good word, we can get ready to start translating to Pig Latin! Let's quickly review the rules for translation:

(1) If the original word starts with a vowel, you append the suffix 'ay' to the end of the word.

Example: anaconda -> anacondaay

(2) If the original word starts with a consonant, you move the first letter of the word to the end, and then append the suffix 'ay'.

Example: python -> ythonpay

Let's create a variable to hold our translation suffix.

Create a variable named pyg and set it equal to the suffix 'ay'.

See the Figure below:

```
script.py
1   pyg='ay'
```

Word Up

Since the translation rules depend on the first letter of the word we are translating, we need to grab it so we can check if it is a consonant or a vowel. To simplify things, we'll also go ahead and make sure that all the letters in our word are lowercase to make things a little easier.

To convert a word to all lowercase letters, we can use `lower()`. For example, to convert the string value `"FOO"` in a variable `x` to lowercase, we could do the following:

```
x = "FOO"
x.lower()  # "foo"
```

You'll want to think about where to put the code that you write in this step. It really only makes sense to do these steps if you already know that you have a useable word, so make sure you put this code **inside** the `if/else` block.

Instruction:

1. Convert the variable original to all lowercase letters. Store the result in a variable named word.
2. Create a new variable called first that holds the first letter of word.

The code will go like this:

```
script.py
1  pyg = 'ay'
2
3  original = raw_input('Enter a word:')
4  original=original.lower()
5  word=original.lower()
6  first=word[0]
7  if len(original) > 0 and original.isalpha():
8      print original
9  else:
10     print 'empty'
```

Note: This code will change your word to lower case. From 'Anaconda' to 'anaconda'.

74

E-I-E-I-O

Now that we have access to the first letter of our word, we need to check to see if it is a vowel or a consonant. Since there are *way* fewer vowels than consonants, it is easier to explicitly check for a vowel. (The vowels in English are: a, e, i, o and u.)

Again, it only makes sense to do this check if we already know that we have a "good" word (one that isn't empty and is all alphabetical characters). You have a couple of options on how to organize your code.

You could add onto your existing `if` condition to check that something is a good word **and** starts with a vowel. But then you'd have to add an `elif` to check if the word is a good word **and** starts with a consonant.

In this case, it makes more sense to **nest** the new `if` block inside the `if` part of the existing if/else. This means that the whole if/else that you will create here goes inside the `if` part of your existing if/else block.

A nested if/else looks like this:

```
if condition:
    if other_condition:
        # Do something
    else:
        # Do something else!
else:
    # Do yet another thing
```

Instruction:

Add a new if/else block nested inside of your existing one.

The new if should check to see if the first letter of word is a vowel. If it is, your code should print "vowel". If the first letter of word is *not* a vowel, your code should print "consonant".

You can remove the print original line from your code.

Your code will go like this:

```
script.py
1   pyg = 'ay'
2
3   original = raw_input('Enter a word:')
4   original=original.lower()
5   word=original.lower()
6   first=word[0]
7   vowel="a,e,i,o,u"
8   if first == "a" or first == "e" or first == "i" or first == "o" or first == "u":
9       print "vowel"
10  else:
11      print "consonant"
```

Note: Now your code will be able to differentiate between vowels and consonants. When you will enter vowel it will return value like this:

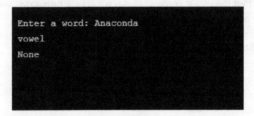

```
Enter a word: Anaconda
vowel
None
```

When you will enter a consonant the code will return value like this:

```
Enter a word: Planet
consonant
None
```

I'd Like to Buy a Vowel

Now that we have the logical structure in place to check for a vowel, let's put in the code to do the actual translation.

Remember that if a word starts with a vowel, you translate it to Pig Latin by appending our suffix ("ay") to the end of the word.

We'll want to make sure we output the result of the translation so we can check our work.

Instruction:

Create a new variable called new_word that contains the result of appending 'ay' to the end of word. (Remember that this suffix is stored in the variable pyg.)

Make sure you are only doing this in the case where the word starts with a vowel. Don't worry about the consonants just yet, we'll get to them in the next step!

After the translation, print the new word so you can check your work. (This should replace the print 'vowel' bit of your code.) Make sure to test your code with a word that starts with a vowel!

Your code will go like this:

```
script.py

1   pyg = 'ay'
2
3   original = raw_input('Enter a word:')
4   word = original.lower()
5   first = word [0]
6   new_word = word + pyg
7   if len(original) > 0 and original.isalpha():
8       if first == 'a' or first == 'e' or first == 'i' or first == 'o' or first == 'u' :
9           print new_word
10  else:
11      print "empty"
```

Now your code will add the suffix 'ay' at the end of word starting with vowels like shown below:

```
Enter a word: Anaconda
anacondaay
None
```

Almost Oneday!

Now that we have the vowel case working, all that's left is to tackle the consonant case (our inner `else`, since a letter can only be a consonant or a vowel).

The rule for translation here is a little trickier. You have to remove the first letter from the word, move it to the end, and then append the 'ay' suffix.

The most appropriate way to get the remainder of the string after removing the first letter is to use *slicing*. If you have a string `s`, you can get the "slice" of `s` from `i` to `j` using `s[i:j]`. This gives you the characters from position `i` to `j`.

For example, if `s = "foo"`, then `s[0:2]` gives you `"fo"`. Think about how to use this technique to get the rest of the string minus the first character.

Instruction:

Inside the `else` part of your if/else block that checks the first letter of the word, set the new_word variable equal to the translation result for a word that starts with a consonant.

Replace the print 'consonant 'bit with print new_word. Make sure to test your code with a word that starts with a consonant!

Your code will go like this:

```
script.py
1  pyg = 'ay'
2
3  original = raw_input('Enter a word:')
4  word=original.lower()
5  first=word[0]
6  new_word = word + pyg
7  if len(original) > 0 and original.isalpha():
8      if first== "a" or first== "e" or first== "i" or first== "o" or first== "u":
9          print new_word
10     else:
11         new_word = original[1:] + original[0:1] + pyg
12         print new_word
13 else:
14     print 'empty'
```

Now you will be able to add suffix 'ay' at the end of vowels like this:

```
Enter a word: Anaconda
anacondaay
None
```

And also to move the first letter of consonant word to the last and to add suffix 'ay' at the end of that like shown below:

```
Enter a word: planet
lanetpay
None
```

With this final code you will get the "empty" value for numerical inputs like shown below:

```
Enter a word: 2345678
empty
None
```

Testing, Testing, is This Thing On?

Yay! You should have a fully functioning Pig Latin translator. Just to make sure everything is working smoothly, make sure you test your code thoroughly.

You'll also want to go back through and take out any print statements that you were using to help debug intermediate steps of your code. While you're cleaning things up—now might be a good time to add some comments too! Making sure your code is clean, commented, and fully functional is just as important as writing it in the first place.

Take a look at your final code again:

```
script.py
1  pyg = 'ay'
2
3  original = raw_input('Enter a word:')
4  word=original.lower()
5  first=word[0]
6  new_word = word + pyg
7  if len(original) > 0 and original.isalpha():
8      if first== "a" or first== "e" or first== "i" or first== "o" or first== "u":
9          print new_word
10     else:
11         new_word = original[1:] + original[0:1] + pyg
12         print new_word
13 else:
14     print 'empty'
```

Now validate your code by inputting different values and see if it serves your purpose. With this code you should be able to translate any text in to Pyg Latin and to get empty value for all other numerical inputs. Check it by giving different inputs now and validate your final project.

DAY-7

FUNCTIONS

Documentation: a PSA

You can use Codecademy as a great educational tool—you can think of it as an online classroom for learning a programming language. It's important to remember, however, that the emphasis should be on you *rapproach* to problems and learning to think like a programmer, and not on memorizing every single method or nuance of syntax to be found in a given programming language.

Think of it this way: if you're going to Germany, you wouldn't say to yourself, "Hey, I took a year of German in college, I don't need my dictionary or translation app!" You would *totally* bring those things to help remind you of vocabulary and syntax in case you were to get stuck; even *professional translators* keep dictionaries and grammar guides handy for unusual words and tricky constructions.

Much like professional translators, professional programmers refer to **documentation** when they're not clear on best practices, forget how a certain method works, or need to look up syntax. Python's documentation can be found docs.python.org. We encourage you to read through it on your own!

Important note for advanced students: Here we are using Python 2.7. This version of Python is the most stable and widely used version of Python. However, in 2008 a new version of Python was created called Python 3. Python 2.7 is considered more stable and is more widely used than Python 3 because there are so many libraries that were created specifically for Python 2. In the past few years, Python 3 has gained more support and is more widely used. Both Python 2.7 and Python 3 are still supported and developed.

Instruction:

Part of Python's documentation are the PEPs, or "Python Enhancement Proposals." PEP 20, "The Zen of Python," is something of an easter egg hidden in the interpreter (you may have caught us quoting from it in instructional text or hints).

Type import this in the editor to see what happens (we'll learn about the import keyword later in this lesson). Scroll to read all the text output to the console. See Figure below:

```
script.py

1  import this
```

It will import like this:

```
Beautiful is better than ugly.
Explicit is better than implicit.
Simple is better than complex.
Complex is better than complicated.
Flat is better than nested.
Sparse is better than dense.
Readability counts.
Special cases aren't special enough to break the rules.
Although practicality beats purity.
Errors should never pass silently.
Unless explicitly silenced.
In the face of ambiguity, refuse the temptation to guess.
There should be one-- and preferably only one --obvious way to do it.
Although that way may not be obvious at first unless you're Dutch.
Now is better than never.
Although never is often better than *right* now.
If the implementation is hard to explain, it's a bad idea.
If the implementation is easy to explain, it may be a good idea.
Namespaces are one honking great idea -- let's do more of those!
None
```

What Good are Functions?

A **function** is a reusable section of code written to perform a specific task in a program. You might be wondering why you need to separate your code into functions, rather than just writing everything out in one giant block. You might have guessed the answer(s) already, but here are some of the big ones:

1. If something goes wrong in your code, it's much easier to find and fix bugs if you've organized your program well. Assigning specific tasks to separate functions helps with this organization.

2. By assigning specific tasks to separate functions (an idea computer scientists call **separation of concerns**), you make your program less redundant and your code more reusable—not only can you repeatedly use the same function in a single program without rewriting it each time, but you can even use that function in *another* program.

3. When we learn more about **objects**, you'll find out there are a lot of interesting things we can do with functions that belong to those objects (called **methods**).

4. D.R.Y. stands for **Don't Repeat Yourself**. Using functions we can avoid repeating ourselves more easily.

5. Recursion is a powerful tool. It allows us to call a piece of code multiple times and call itself. There are some programming problems that cannot be solved without recursion! Functions make it possible to do recursion.

Instruction:

Check out the code in the editor. If you completed the Tip Calculator project, you'll remember going through and calculating tax and tip in one chunk of program. Here you can see we've defined two functions: tax to calculate the tax on a bill, and tip to compute the tip.

See how much of the code you understand at first glance (we'll explain it all soon). See Figure:

```
script.py

1  def tax(bill):
2      """Adds 8% tax to a restaurant bill."""
3      bill *= 1.08
4      print "With tax: %f" % bill
5      return bill
6
7  def tip(bill):
8      """Adds 15% tip to a restaurant bill."""
9      bill *= 1.15
10     print "With tip: %f" % bill
11     return bill
12
13  meal_cost = 100
14  meal_with_tax = tax(meal_cost)
15  meal_with_tip = tip(meal_with_tax)
```

This code will return the values of meal inclusive of tax and tip as shown below:

```
With tax: 108.000000
With tip: 124.200000
None
```

Ample Examples

All right! Now that you know what functions are good for, it's time to see one in action. (Hopefully it's familiar to you!)

You'll see in the editor a variable, `length`, assigned to the **result** or **output** of a function, `len()`. This function is built into Python (we'll see how to define our own functions in a moment—you got a sneak peek in the last exercise). Here's how the code to the right works:

1. It first evaluates the right hand-side of the assignment. To evaluate the function call, it looks at the long string in parentheses.

2. Since it's a string literal, it doesn't need to be evaluated (that is, it's not an expression that Python has to figure out, like `1 + 1`). So, this string is fed directly as an input to the `len()` function.

3. `len()` accepts this **input** and **returns** (or **outputs**) an integer representing the length of the literal string (in this case `45`, including spaces and punctuation).

   We've tossed in a `print` statement to show you that the result is, in fact, `45`.

Instruction:

Replace the string literal inside len's parentheses with a stringified version of the number `45`. That is, don't just type `"45"`, but actually use a string function to turn 45 into a string.

See Figure below:

```
script.py
1  length = len(str(45))
2  print length
```

This code will turn the digit 45 into string and will generate the length of string.

Function Junction

Functions are defined using the keyword `def` (short for "define"). Functions have three parts:

1. The **header**, which includes the `def` keyword, the name of the function, any **parameters** the function takes inside parentheses (`()`), and a colon (`:`). (We'll get to parameters in the next exercise);

2. An optional **docstring**, which is a triple-quoted, multi-line comment that *briefly* explains what the function does;

3. And the **body**, which is the code block that describes the procedures the function carries out. The body is indented (much like for `if`, `elif`, and `else` statements).

Here's an example of what the syntax would look like for a simple function, `ni_sayer`, that just prints "Ni!" to the console:

```
def ni_sayer():
    """Prints 'Ni!' to the console."""
    print "Ni!"
```

(This is not a very good example of a docstring—ideally, the docstring should explain something that isn't blindingly obvious.)

Instruction:

Time for you to make your own simple function. Go ahead and create a function, spam, that prints the string "Eggs!" to the console. Be sure to use the capitalization and punctuation shown! Don't forget to include a docstring of your own choosing (just remember to enclose it in triple quotes). Your code should go like this and should print "Eggs!" as out put.

```
script.py

1   # Define your spam function starting on line 5. You
2   # can leave the code on line 11 alone for now--we'll
3   # explain it soon!
4
5   def spam():
6       """Prints "Eggs!" to the console."""
7       print "Eggs!"
8
9
10
11
12  # Define the spam function above this line.
13  spam()
```

Call and Response

Defining a function is all well and good, but it's not much use to you unless you **call** it. That's the code you saw on line 11 in the previous exercise: when Python saw `spam()`, it understood that to mean: "Look for the function called `spam` and execute the code inside it." The parentheses after the function name let Python know that `spam` is the name of a function.

Instruction:

We've set up a function, square, (see figure below). Call it on the number 10 on line 9 to see what it does! (That is, put 10between the parentheses of square().)

```
script.py

1 · def square(n):
2       """Returns the square of a number."""
3       squared = n**2
4       print "%d squared is %d." % (n, squared)
5       return squared
6
7 # Call the square function on line 9! Make sure to
8 # include the number 10 between the parentheses.
9 square(10)
10
```

You will get the square value of 10 (i.e. 100) like shown below:

```
10 squared is 100.
None
```

No One Ever Does

If a function takes **arguments**, we say it **accepts** or **expects** those arguments. For instance, if the function no_one takes a single argument, "The Spanish Inquisition", we would say that no_one **expects** "The Spanish Inquisition".

Ha!

To be precise, the **argument** is the piece of code you actually put between the function's parentheses when you **call** it, and the **parameter** is the name you put between the function's parentheses when you **define** it. For instance, when we defined square in the previous exercise, we gave it the parameter n (for "number"), but **passed** it the argument 10 when we **called** it.

You can think of parameters as nicknames the function definition gives to arguments, since it doesn't know ahead of time exactly what argument it's going to get.

The syntax for a function that just prints out the argument it expects would look something like the below.

Function definition:

```
def no_one(sentence):
    print sentence
```

Calling the function:

```
no_one("The Spanish Inquisition")
```

And the console would display:

```
"The Spanish Inquisition"
```

which is the value the parameter sentence takes on when you call no_one and pass the argument "The Spanish Inquisition".

Instruction:

Make sense? Good! Check out the function, power. It should take two arguments, a base and an exponent, and raise the first to the power of the second. It's currently broken, however, because its parameters are missing.

Replace the ___s with the parameters base and exponent and call power on a base of 37 and a power of 4. See Figures below:

```
script.py
1   def power(___, ___):  # Add your parameters here!
2       result = base**exponent
3       print "%d to the power of %d is %d." % (base, exponent, result)
4
5   power(___,___)  # Add your arguments here!
```

Now fill in the spaces like this:

```
script.py
1   def power(base, exponent):  # Add your parameters here!
2       result = base**exponent
3       print "%d to the power of %d is %d." % (base, exponent, result)
4
5   power(37,4)  # Add your arguments here!
```

You will get 37 to the power of 4 like shown in figure below:

```
37 to the power of 4 is 1874161.
None
```

Splat!

Speaking of not knowing what to expect: your functions not only don't know what arguments they're going to get ahead of time, but occasionally, they don't even know *how many* arguments there will be.

Let's say you have a function, `favorite_actor`, that `prints` out the argument it receives from the user. It might look something like this:

```
def favorite_actor(name):
    """Prints out your favorite actor."""
    print "Favorite actor is: " + name
```

This is great for just one actor, but what if you want to print out the user's favorite actor**s**, without knowing how many names the user will put in?

The solution: **splat arguments**. Splat arguments are an arbitrary number of arguments, and you use them by preceding your parameter with a *. This says to Python, "Hey man, I don't know *how* many arguments there are about to be, but it could be more than one." The convention is to use *args, but you can use just about any name you like with a* before it.

Instruction:

Replace the _____s in the function to the right with the appropriate code and click Save & Submit Code to see who your favorite actors are (or, at least, who they *should* be). Remember to include a * before your parameter (between the parentheses on line 1).

You don't need the * when you replace the _____ on line 3—just the parameter name you chose on line 1.

See Figures below:

```
script.py

1 - def favorite_actors(_____):
2       """Prints out your favorite actorS (plural!)"""
3       print "Your favorite actors are:" , _____
4
5
6   favorite_actors("Michael Palin", "John Cleese", "Graham Chapman")
```

Now fill in the blank spaces like this:

```
script.py

1  def favorite_actors(*name):
2      """Prints out your favorite actorS (plural!)"""
3      print "Your favorite actors are:" , name
4
5
6  favorite_actors("Michael Palin", "John Cleese", "Graham Chapman")
```

You will see that by using *name you will be able to get the names of all your favorite actors at once as shown in figure below:

```
Your favorite actors are: ('Michael Palin', 'John Cleese', 'Graham Chapman')
None
```

Now by using the Splat method you will be able to get more than one values altogether just by defining the name value with * in parameter that will call the values defined in argument and will display them in a single place.

Functions Calling Functions

So far, we've seen functions that can print text to the console or do simple arithmetic, but functions can be much more powerful than that. For example, it's completely permissible for a function to call another function. In order to call a function within another function, just call the function. Like so:

```
def fun_one(n):
    return n * 5

def fun_two(m):
    return fun_one(m) + 7
```

Instruction:

Check out the two functions in the editor: one_good_turn and deserves_another. The first function adds 1 to number it gets as an argument, and the second adds 2.

In the body of deserves_another, change the function so that it always adds 2 to the output of one_good_turn. See Figure below:

Value of one_good_turn will be set like this:

Practice Makes Perfect

You never really know how to do something until you do it yourself. We're taking the training wheels off now: time for you to define and call functions all on your lonesome.

You can always practice your functions (or any Python code) in your interpreter or alternatively at the Codecademy Labs. Experimenting in the Labs is a great way to reinforce what you've learned so far.

Instruction:

1. Define a function called cube that takes a number and returns the cube of that number. (Cubing a number is the same as raising it to the third power).
2. Define a second function called by_three that takes one number as an argument. If that number is evenly divisible by 3, by_three should call cube on that number. If the number is not evenly divisible by 3, by_three should return False.

So, for example, by_three should take 9, determine it's evenly divisible by 3, and pass it to cube, who returns 729 (the result of 9**3). If by_three gets 4, however, it should return False and leave it at that.

Your code should go like this:

```
script.py
1  def cube(n):
2      return n**3
3  def by_three(n):
4      if n%3:
5          return False
6      else:
7          return cube(n)
8  m = raw_input('Enter an integer')
9  try:
10     n = int(m)
11     print by_three(n)
12 except ValueError:
13     print("That's not an int!")
```

If you enter the value of 3 in the pop up box you should get the cube of 3 (i.e. 27) as shown in figure below:

```
Enter an integer 3
27
None
```

In case you enter any digit other than 3 you should get the False value as shown below:

```
Enter an integer 4
False
None
```

The code shown above is just for setting up an example for you. You can write your own code containing 'if', 'elif', 'else' conditions and can set your own parameters and arguments for this purpose. Remember that just practice will maketh you perfect so try to do as much practice as you can.

I Know Kung Fu

Remember `import this` from the first exercise in this course? That was an example of **import**ing a **module**. A module is a file that contains definitions—including variables and functions—that you can use. It would clutter up the interpreter to keep all these variables and functions around all the time, so you just `import` the module you want when you need something from it.

Instruction:

Before we try any fancy importing, let's see what Python already knows about square roots. On line 3 in the editor, ask Python to

print sqrt(25)

which we would expect to equal five.

See Figure below:

```
script.py

1  # Ask Python to print sqrt(25) on line 3.
2
3  print sqrt(25)
```

Note: You need not to get worried if you don't get 5 but get some error. The reason for this will be explained on next pages.

Generic Imports

Did you see that? Python said: "NameError: name 'sqrt' is not defined." Python doesn't know what square roots are—yet.

There is a Python module named `math` that includes a number of useful variables and functions, and (as you've probably guessed) `sqrt()` is one of those functions. In order to get to it, all you need is the `import` keyword. When you simply import a module this way, it's called a **generic import**.

Instruction:

You'll need to do two things here:

1. Type import math on line 2in the editor, and
2. Insert math. (that's math, followed by a period) before sqrt(). This tells Python not only to import math, but to get the sqrt() function from within math.

Once you've done this, hit "run" to see what Python now knows.

See Figure below:

```
script.py

1  # Ask Python to print sqrt(25) on line 3.
2  import math
3  print math.sqrt(25)
```

As you have told the Python that what exactly you want it to do, you will get the answer like this:

```
5.0
None
```

Function Imports

Nice work! Now Python knows how to take the square root of a number (as well as how to do everything contained in the `math` module).

Importing the entire `math` module is kind of annoying for two reasons, though: first, we really only want the `sqrt` function, and second, we have to remember to type `math.sqrt()` any time we want to retrieve that function from the `math` module.

Thankfully, it's possible to import only certain variables or functions from a given module. Pulling in just a single function from a module is called a **function import**, and it's done using the `from` keyword, like so:

```
from module import function
```

where "module" and "function" are replaced by the names of the module and function you want. The best part is, now you only have to type `sqrt()` to get the square root of a number—no more `math.sqrt()`!

Instruction:

Let's import the sqrt function from math again, only this time, let's only get the sqrt function. (You don't need the () after sqrt in the from math import sqrt bit.) See Figure below:

```
script.py
1  # Import *just* the sqrt function from math on line 3!
2
3  from math import sqrt
```

The value of this from math import function is great. By using this function you will be able to import the math tool you need rater than importing the whole tool box that is of no use. This import function will let you perform the mathematical calculations with ease and you will need not to specify math.name.

Universal Imports

Great! We've found a way to handpick the variables and functions we want from the modules that contain them.

What if we want a large selection (or *all*) of the variables and functions available in a module? We can `import module`, but there's another option.

When you `import math`, you're basically saying: "Bring the Math Box to my apartment so I can use all the cool stuff in it." Whenever you want a tool in `math`, you have to go to the box and pull out the thing you want (which is why you have to type `math.name` for everything—even though the box is in your apartment, all the cool stuff you want is still in that box).

When you choose `from math import sqrt`, you're saying: "Bring me *only* the square root tool from the Math Box, and don't bring the Math Box to my apartment." This means you can use `sqrt` without reference to `math`, but if you want anything else from `math`, you have to import it separately, since the whole Math Box isn't in your apartment for you to dig through.

The third option is to say: "Don't bring the Math Box to my apartment, but bring me *absolutely every tool in it*." This gives you the advantage of having a wide variety of tools, and since you have them in your apartment and they're not all still stuck in the Math Box, you don't have to constantly type `math.name` to get what you want.

The syntax for this is:

```
from module import *
```

If you're familiar with CSS, you've seen that * can stand for "every selector," and it serves a similar function in Python: it stands in for every variable and function name in a module.

Instruction:

Use the power of from module import * to import everything from the math module on line 3 of the editor.

See Figure below:

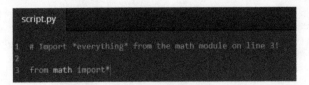

Here Be Dragons

Here's something we've learned in life (and not just from programming): just because you can do something doesn't mean that you *should*.

Universal imports may look great on the surface, but they're not a good idea for one very important reason: they can fill your program with a *ton* of variable and function names, but without the safety of those names still being associated with the module(s) they came from.

If you have a function of your very own named `sqrt` and you `import math`, your function is safe: there is your `sqrt` and there is `math.sqrt`, and ne'er the twain shall meet. If you do `from math import *`, however, you have a problem: namely, two different functions with the exact same name.

Even if your own definitions don't directly conflict with names from imported modules, if you `import *` from several modules at once, there won't be any way for you to figure out which variable or function came from where. It'd be like having someone dump a ton of random stuff from a bunch of different boxes in your apartment, then throwing the boxes away so you can't even see where the stuff came from.

For these reasons, it's best to stick with either `import module` and suffer the inconvenience of having to type `module.name`, or just `import` specific variables and functions from various modules as needed.

Instruction:

Line 1 and line 3 in the editor should look familiar to you; line 2 is an example of some of the cool stuff you'll be able to do in future lessons. In a nutshell, this code will show you everything available in the math module.

Submit Code to check it out (you'll see sqrt, along with some other useful things like pi, factorial, and trigonometric functions). Feel free to spend a few minutes playing around with them!

See Figures below:

```
script.py
1  import math              # Imports the math module
2  everything = dir(math)   # Sets everything to a list of things from math
3  print everything         # Prints 'em all!
```

After submitting this code in your editor you will import all mathematical functions/values like shown below:

```
['__doc__', '__name__', '__package__', 'acos', 'acosh', 'asin', 'asinh', 'atan', 'atan2',
'atanh', 'ceil', 'copysign', 'cos', 'cosh', 'degrees', 'e', 'erf', 'erfc', 'exp',
'expm1', 'fabs', 'factorial', 'floor', 'fmod', 'frexp', 'fsum', 'gamma', 'hypot',
'isinf', 'isnan', 'ldexp', 'lgamma', 'log', 'log10', 'log1p', 'modf', 'pi', 'pow',
'radians', 'sin', 'sinh', 'sqrt', 'tan', 'tanh', 'trunc']
None
```

Now you will feel yourself at much ease as compared to all other programmers. Python has imported all math tools for you and you will be able to perform whatsoever mathematical function you want to and that too without importing tools again and again and without mentioning math.name while performing calculations.

Now you can tell Python that what you want to do and it will get it done for you. Python is the language that will make you think like a Computer Scientist by increasing your power to solve the problems and to get easy and simplified solutions for all problems.

On Beyond Strings

Now that you understand what functions are and how to import modules, it's worth showing you some of the cool functions that are built in to Python (no modules required!).

You already know about some of the built-in functions we've used on (or to create) strings, such as `.upper()`, `.lower()`, `str()`, and `len()`. These are great for doing work with strings, but what about something a little more analytic?

Instruction:

Check out the code in the editor. What do you think it'll do? Check it yourself when you think you have an idea.

See Figure below:

```
script.py

1  def biggest_number(*args):
2      print max(args)
3      return max(args)
4
5  def smallest_number(*args):
6      print min(args)
7      return min(args)
8
9  def distance_from_zero(arg):
10     print abs(arg)
11     return abs(arg)
12
13
14  biggest_number(-10, -5, 5, 10)
15  smallest_number(-10, -5, 5, 10)
16  distance_from_zero(-10)
```

Note: This code should be able to print the biggest and smallest number and to print the distance of numbers from zero.

max()

The max() function takes any number of arguments and returns the largest one. ("Largest" can have odd definitions here, so it's best to use max() on things like integers and floats, where the results are straightforward, and not on other objects, like strings.)

For example, max(1,2,3) will return 3 (the largest number in the set of arguments).

Instruction:

Try out the max() function on line 3 of the editor. You can provide any number of integer or float arguments to max().

See Figure below:

```
script.py

1  # Set maximum to the max value of any set of numbers on line 3!
2
3  maximum = max(4,10,8,3)
4
5  print maximum
```

With this maximum code you should be able to print the value of maximum number (i.e. the Largest number from within the specified string. In this example the value of print should be 10.

min()

As you might imagine, `min()` does the opposite of `max()`—given a series of arguments, it returns the smallest one.

Instruction:

Go ahead and set minimum equal to the min() of any set of integers or floats you'd like.

See Figure below:

```
script.py
1  # Set minimum to the min value of any set of numbers on line 3!
2
3  minimum = min(5,3,8,9,11,20,1,0)
4
5  print minimum
```

With this maximum code you should be able to print the value of minimum number (i.e. the Smallest number from within the specified string. In this example the value of print should be 0.

abs()

The abs() function returns the **absolute value** of the number it takes as an argument—that is, that number's distance from 0 on an imagined number line, regardless of whether it's positive or negative. For instance, 3 and -3 are both equally far from 0, and thus have the same absolute value: 3. The abs() function always returns a positive value, and unlike max() and min(), it can only take a single number.

Instruction:

Set absolute equal to the absolute value of -42 on line 2. (This may seem basic, but bear with us—you'll see the value of the exercise soon enough.)

See Figure below:

```
script.py
1
2  absolute = abs(-42)
3
4  print absolute
```

This abs() function will return you the absolute value of a value specified. In our case the specified value is -42 so the print will return the absolute value of 42.

type()

Finally, the `type()` function does something very interesting: it returns the **type** of the data it receives as an argument. If you ask Python to do the following:

```
print type(42)
print type(4.2)
print type('spam')
print type({'Name':'John Cleese'})
print type((1,2))
```

Python will output:

```
<type 'int'>
<type 'float'>
<type 'unicode'>
<type 'dict'>
<type 'tuple'>
```

(The 'unicode' type is a special type of string.)

You're already familiar with `integers`, `floats`, and `strings`; you'll learn about `dictionaries` and `tuples` in later lessons.

Instruction:

Have Python print out the type of an int, a float, and a unicode string in the editor. You can pick any values on which to call type(), so long as they produce one of each.

See Figure below:

```
script.py
1  # Print out the types of an integer, a float,
2  # and a string on separate lines below.
3  print type(21)
4  print type (3.1)
5  print type ('consonant')
```

It will give you the type of values like this:

```
<type 'int'>
<type 'float'>
<type 'str'>
None
```

Review: Functions

Up until now, the review section of each unit has been a single exercise. As you progress through the Python courses, you'll see longer review sections (starting with this one)—this is to ensure you have ample practice as you're exposed to more (and more complex) aspects of the language.

Okay! Let's review functions. Again, training wheels are off, but feel free to take a peek at earlier exercises if you need a refresher.

Instruction:

Write a function, shut_down, that takes one parameter (you can use anything you like; in this case, we'd use s for string). The shut_down function should return "Shutting down..."when it gets "Yes", "yes", or "YES" as an argument, and "Shutdown aborted!" when it gets "No", "no", or "NO".

If it gets anything other than those inputs, the function should return "Sorry, I didn't understand you."

You don't need to specify the raw_input for this function. Just write function to perform shutdown task.

Your function could be something like this:

```python
def shut_down(argument):
    if argument.lower() == "yes":
        return "Shutting down..."
    elif argument.lower() == "no":
        return "Shutdown aborted!"
    else:
        return "Sorry, I didn't understand you."

print shut_down("yes")
```

You should write your own function and should validate it by executing it in the interpreter.

Review: Modules

Good work! Now let's see what you remember about importing modules (and, specifically, what's available in the `math` module).

Instruction:

Import the math module in whatever way you prefer. Call its sqrt function on the number13689 and print that value to the console.

Code could be something like this:

```
script.py
1  from math import sqrt
2  print sqrt(13689)
```

Again, write your own function and validate it by executing it in the interpreter.

Review: Built-In Functions

Perfect! Last but not least, let's review some of the built-in functions you've learned about in this lesson.

Instruction:

This is a two-parter: first, define a function, distance_from_zero, with one parameter (choose any parameter name you like).

Second, have that function do the following:

1. Check the type of the input it receives.
2. If the type is int or float, the function should return the absolute value of the function input.
3. If the type is any other type, the function should return "Not an integer or float!"

It could be something like this:

```
script.py
1  def distance_from_zero(n):
2      if type(n) == int or type(n) == float:
3          return abs(n)
4      else:
5          return "Not an integer or float!"
```

Once again, write your own function and validate it by checking the type of integers and words through print type() command in the interpreter.

DAY-8

TRIP PLANNING CALCULATOR

Before We Begin

Before we start the lesson, we are just going to do a quick review of functions in Python. Remember, functions are callable blocks of code that we can use over and over again. Using functions saves us time, lines of code, and confusion when writing long programs.

Instruction:

For a warm up, write a function called answer that takes no input and returns the value 42.

The code could be something like this:

```
script.py
1   def answer():
2       answer=42
3       return answer
```

You must keep in your mind that the code should 'return' not 'print' the answer.

Finding Your Identity

Unfortunately for us, 42 is not the answer to every question in the universe.

Instruction:

Write the function identity that takes the input x and returns x. You do not need to call the function.

See Figure below:

```
script.py

1  def identity(x):
2      if identity(x):
3          return "x"
```

Once again you should write the code in a way that it could 'return' not 'print' the answer. You should remember that 'return' is just like a math function call, the function call will evaluate into what is returned - if nothing is specified (even if there is no return) the function will return None by default in python.

Call Me Maybe?

Remember that you can call functions to make computationally challenging tasks much easier.

Instruction:

Call the function cube with an input of 27 on line 4. Print the result to the console. Your code could be something like this:

```
script.py

1  def cube(x):
2      return x**3
3
4  print cube(27)
```

This code will return the cube of 27 as shown below:

```
19683
None
```

In the above example we defined the parameter and then again at line 4 we set the argument for that parameter and asked the python to return the defined values by printing them subsequently. Hence now Python will not return 'None' but will return the calculated value for the argument set for the defined parameter.

Function and Control Flow

Remember that functions often have to react differently depending on the input they receive.

Instruction:

Write a function called is_even that takes one input, x, and returns the string "yep" if the input is even and "nope" otherwise. You do not need to call the function.

See Figure below:

```
script.py

1   def is_even(x):
2       if x % 2 == 0 :
3           return "yep"
4       else:
5           return "nope"
```

The right function should return the result "None" when asking only for return. If you want to validate the working of function to check that whether it returns "yep" for even and "nope" for all other inputs, you can check it by giving the print command by specifying the argument for is_even like print is_even(11) and could validate results for different inputs.

Problem Solvers

This final review exercise will involve applying functions to a real life problem.

Let's try writing a function to solve a traditional math question.

For this exercise, you'll need to import the `math` module discussed in Unit 4. This can be achieved by typing `import math` at the top of your program.

Instruction:

Write a function called area_of_circle that takes radius as input and returns the area of a circle. The area of a circle is equal to pi times the radius squared. (Use the math.pi in order to represent Pi.)

A simple function could be something like this:

```
script.py
1  import math
2  def area_of_circle(r):
3      return r ** 2 * math.pi
```

Planning Your Trip

When planning a vacation, it is very important to know exactly how much you are going to spend. With the aid of programming, this task becomes very easy.

We will break your trip down into 3 main costs and then put them together in one big function at the end.

Instruction:

First, write a function called hotel_cost that takes the variable nights as input. The function should return how much you have to pay if the hotel costs 140 dollars for every night that you stay. See Figure below:

```
script.py

1 - def hotel_cost(nights):
2       return nights * 140
```

A successful function will return "None" upon execution. But if you are going for a big project involving a lengthy code you can divide your code in several steps and could validate each step for its authenticity. If you want to see that whether this function will perform the right calculation for you or not, you can check it by entering the following few lines after your code. Now your code will perform calculation for 5 days stay and will print the amount of bill for you.

```
script.py

1 - def hotel_cost(nights):
2       return nights * 140
3   bill=hotel_cost (1)
4 - def get_min(balance,rate):
5       return balance*rate
6   print get_min(bill,5)
```

Getting There

To get to your location, you are going to need to take a plane ride.

Instruction:

Below your existing code, write a function called plane_ride_cost that takes a string, city, as input. The function should return a different price depending on the location. Below are the valid destinations and their corresponding round-trip prices.

1. "Charlotte": 183
2. "Tampa": 220
3. "Pittsburgh": 222
4. "Los Angeles": 475

See Figure below for sample code:

```
script.py

1  def hotel_cost(nights):
2      return nights * 140
3
4  def plane_ride_cost(city):
5      if city=="Charlotte":
6          return 183
7      if city=="Tampa":
8          return 220
9      if city=="Pittsburgh":
10         return 222
11     if city=="Los Angeles":
12         return 475
```

To validate your code you can check the total cost of trip by entering these lines below your code:

```
14  def trip_cost(city, days):
15      return plane_ride_cost(city) + hotel_cost(days)
16
17  # You were planning on taking a trip to Tampa for five days.
18  expected_cost = trip_cost("Tampa", 7)
19  #print expected_cost
20  over = expected_cost
21  print over
```

It will return total cost of trip for specified days and city.

Transportation

Now when you arrive at your destination, you are going to need a rental car in order for you to get around. Luckily for you, the rental car company you use gives discounts depending on how many days you rent the car.

Instruction:

Below your existing code, write a function called rental_car_cost that takes days as input and returns the cost for renting a car for said number of days. The cost must abide by the following conditions:

1. Every day you rent the car is $40.
2. If you rent the car for 3 or more days, you get $20 off your total.
3. If you rent the car for 7 or more days, you get $50 off your total. (This *does not* stack with the 20 dollars you get for renting the car over 3 days.)

Now the code will seem like this:

```
script.py

1   def hotel_cost(nights):
2       return nights * 140
3   bill=hotel_cost (1)
4   def get_min(balance,rate):
5       return balance*rate
6   print get_min(bill,5)
7   def plane_ride_cost(city):
8       if city=="Charlotte":
9           return 183
10      if city=="Tampa":
11          return 220
12      if city=="Pittsburgh":
13          return 222
14      if city=="Los Angeles":
15          return 475
16  def rental_car_cost(days):
17      if days >= 7:
18          return days * 40 - 50
19      if days in (3,4,5,6,):
20          return days * 40 - 20
21      else:
22          return days * 40
```

Pull it Together

Great! Now that you've got your 3 main costs figured out, it's time to put them together in order to find the total cost of your trip.

Instruction:

Below your existing code, write a function called trip_cost that takes two inputs, city and days. city should be the city that you are going to visit and days should be the number of days that you are staying.

Have your function return the **sum** of the rental_car_cost,hotel_cost, and plane_ride_cost functions with their respective inputs.

Hope you will be remembering the lines you entered for code validation earlier in plane_ride_cost function. You will just alter those lines and will be able to pull all costs together by validating the execution of your code.

See Figure below:

```
script.py

1  def hotel_cost(nights):
2      return 140 * nights
3
4  def plane_ride_cost(city):
5      if city == "Charlotte":
6          return 183
7      elif city == "Tampa":
8          return 220
9      elif city == "Pittsburgh":
10         return 222
11     elif city == "Los Angeles":
12         return 475
13
14 def rental_car_cost(days):
15     cost = days * 40
16     if days >= 7:
17         cost = cost - 50
18     elif days >= 3:
19         cost = cost - 20
20     return cost
21
22 def trip_cost(city, days):
23     return plane_ride_cost(city)+ rental_car_cost(days) + hotel_cost(days)
24
25 # You were planning on taking a trip to Pittsburgh for five days.
26 expected_cost = trip_cost("Pittsburgh", 7)
27 #print expected_cost
28 over = expected_cost
29 print over
```

117

Hey, You Never Know!

You can't expect to only spend money on the plane ride, hotel, and rental car when going on a vacation. While the above items will cover the majority of your expenses, there also needs to be room for additional costs like fancy food or souvenirs.

The amount of money that you wish to spend on additional luxuries is completely up to you.

Instruction:

Make it so that your trip_cost function takes a third parameter, spending_money. Just modify the trip_cost function to do just as it did before, except add the spending money to the total that it returns.

You don't need to add anything in the lines of your main code. Just add spending_money in trip_cost return parameter and add the amount in expected_cost like this:

```
22  def trip_cost(city, days, spending_money):
23      return plane_ride_cost(city)+ rental_car_cost(days) + hotel_cost(days) + spending_money
24
25  # You were planning on taking a trip to Los Angeles for five days.
26  expected_cost = trip_cost("Los Angeles", 7, 500)
27  #print expected_cost
28  over = expected_cost
29  print over
```

It will add the additional amount in your total expected cost. You can validate it by executing your code with different inputs.

Grand Finale Exercise

Now that you have it all together, print out the cost of a trip to "Los Angeles" for 5 days with an extra 600 dollars of spending money.

We are leaving this space blank in wait of your code...............

Coming Back Home

Welcome back home! It looks like you've had an amazing vacation.

Unfortunately for you, one too many drinks and a bit too much time at the casino have put you a bit over-budget.

Instruction:

Go ahead and print out how far over budget you went if you spent 2734.23 on your trip. You can deduct this amount from your total bill and may come with something like this:

```
25   # You were planning on taking a trip to Los Angeles.
26   # for five days with $600 of spending money.
27   print 2734.23-trip_cost("Los Angeles", 5, 600)
```

In this way you will be able to deduct any extra spending from your total estimated cost and will get the exact amount of extra spending. Keep in your mind that if you will deduct this amount from trip_cost by performing the deduction function like trip_cost-extra_spending you will get negative number that may seem odd for you, so performing the function like extra_spending-trip_cost will return a positive number and is the best acceptable way to perform calculations in Python.

The result of this code will be like this and Python will accept this result as well otherwise it will return error message specifying that the result is not what it should be:

Gotta Give Me Some Credit

Yikes! That is a bit more than you intended to spend. You put your hotel bill on your credit card and now you don't have the money to pay for it up front.

It looks like you're going to have to break it up into monthly payments. Programming might aid you in handling this mess.

Instruction:

Call the hotel_cost function with 5 nights as the input and store the result in a variable called bill.

Simply you can do this in the following way:

```
script.py
1  def hotel_cost(nights):
2      return nights * 140
3  bill= hotel_cost(5)
```

If you want to validate the execution of your code, just add print bill in your code and it will return the amount of bill according to specified parameters and arguments. See Figure below:

```
script.py
1  def hotel_cost(nights):
2      return nights * 140
3  bill= hotel_cost(5)
4  print bill
```

At a Bare Minimum

First, we need to know what the minimum payment is that you can make each month.

Note that the minimum payment you can make is 2% of your total balance. So the minimum payment you can make with a rate of 2% and a balance of 1,000 would be 20 dollars (1000 * 0.02 equals 20.)

Instruction:

Below your existing code, write a function called get_min that takes balance and rate as inputs (in that order) and returns the minimum payment that you can make with your total balance. balance and rate should both be given as numbers and not percentages, so 2% is 0.02.

Go ahead and print out the minimum payment of your bill with a 2% rate, as calculated by your get_min function.

Your function will go like this:

```
4   def get_minimum(balance, rate):
5       return bill * 0.02
6   print get_minimum(140, 0.02)
```

The new code giving the minimum amount to be paid at the specified rate will go like this:

```
script.py

1   def hotel_cost(nights):
2       return nights * 140
3   bill= hotel_cost(5)
4   def get_minimum(balance, rate):
5       return bill * 0.02
6   print get_minimum(140, 0.02)
```

Something of Interest

All credit cards charge interest in proportion to your current balance. It's important that we know exactly how much we still owe after making a payment.

Instruction:

Write a function called add_monthly_interest that takes the input balance and returns your balance with interest added to it.

Assume your annual interest is 15%. This means that we need to add on 15% to whatever balance is passed in!

Note that 1/12th of your interest multiplied by your balance is equal to the amount of interest you pay each month (or at least close, anyway). So, add *monthly* interest(100) should return 101.25.

In other words, your function should return the balance passed to it plus the monthly interest, which is 0.15/12 times the balance.

The function will be something like this:

```
7 - def add_monthly_interest(balance):
8       return balance * (1 + (0.15 / 12))
9   print add_monthly_interest(100)
```

This function will print the amount of interest at 15% equally divided for 12 months for the specified amount of 100 dollars. Your new code will be like this:

```
script.py

1 - def hotel_cost(nights):
2       return nights * 140
3   bill= hotel_cost(5)
4 - def get_minimum(balance, rate):
5       return bill * 0.02
6   print get_minimum(140, 0.02)
7 - def add_monthly_interest(balance):
8       return balance * (1 + (0.15 / 12))
9   print add_monthly_interest(100)
```

Paying Up

Now it's time for you to make a function that computes how much you still owe after every monthly payment.

You'll create the function `make_payment` as described below. The function should `return` how much you still owe after you make an arbitrary payment at the beginning of the month.

Note: you calculate how much you still owe by subtracting your payment from your total balance and then adding interest using your `add_monthly_interest` function.

Next, we will call our `make_payment` function to try and solve a real world problem. Note that this may be more difficult than what you are used to but we have faith in you!

Instruction:

Finish the function make_payment that takes the inputs payment and balance.

Have the function print the string "You still owe: x", with x being the amount that you still owe. Then return the amount you still owe. Remember to add interest to the final amount!

We went to a hotel for 5 nights. We then decided to pay half the bill. Then we decided to pay another 100 dollars. At the end of your code, make sure to print out how much we still owe.

Your make_payment function will go like this:

```
 8  def make_payment(payment, balance):
 9      after = balance - payment
10      return add_monthly_interest(after)
11
12  new_bill = make_payment(bill / 2, bill)
13  print "You still owe: ", (make_payment(100, new_bill))
```

The whole code will go like this:

```
script.py
1  def hotel_cost(nights):
2      return nights * 140
3  bill = hotel_cost(5)
4
5  def add_monthly_interest(balance):
6      return balance * (1 + (0.15 / 12))
7
8  def make_payment(payment, balance):
9      after = balance - payment
10     return add_monthly_interest(after)
11
12 new_bill = make_payment(bill / 2, bill)
13 print "You still owe: ", (make_payment(100, new_bill))
```

Your code will now return the amount you still owe like this:

```
You still owe:  257.5546875
None
```

Now your trip is over. Run your code, validate its execution and make the payment for your trip. Now is the time to take rest for next day coursework.

DAY-9

PYTHON LISTS AND DICTIONARIES

Introduction to Lists

Lists are a **datatype** you can use to store a collection of different pieces of information as a sequence under a single variable name. (Datatypes you've already learned about include strings, numbers, and booleans.)

You can assign items to a list with an expression of the form

```
list_name = [item_1, item_2]
```

with the items in between brackets. A list can also be empty: `empty_list = []`.
Lists are very similar to strings, but there are a few key differences.

Instruction:

The list zoo_animals has three items (check them out on line 1). Go ahead and add a fourth! Just enter the name of your favorite animal (as a "string") on line 1, after the final comma but before the closing]. See Figure below:

```
script.py

1  zoo_animals = ["pangolin", "cassowary", "sloth", ];
2  # One animal is missing!
3
4  if len(zoo_animals) > 3:
5      print "The first animal at the zoo is the " + zoo_animals[0]
6      print "The second animal at the zoo is the " + zoo_animals[1]
7      print "The third animal at the zoo is the " + zoo_animals[2]
8      print "The fourth animal at the zoo is the " + zoo_animals[3]
```

You will add the fourth animal in the list like this:

```
1  zoo_animals = ["pangolin", "cassowary", "sloth", "lion" ];
```

Now we have added the fourth animal in the list of zoo_animals i.e. "lion". The list will be showing like this now:

```
1  zoo_animals = ["pangolin", "cassowary", "sloth", "lion" ];
2  # One animal is missing!
3
4 ▾ if len(zoo_animals) > 3:
5      print "The first animal at the zoo is the " + zoo_animals[0]
6      print "The second animal at the zoo is the " + zoo_animals[1]
7      print "The third animal at the zoo is the " + zoo_animals[2]
8      print "The fourth animal at the zoo is the " + zoo_animals[3]
```

You should now be able to execute this code successfully to print the list of animals in zoo like shown below:

```
The first animal at the zoo is the pangolin
The second animal at the zoo is the cassowary
The third animal at the zoo is the sloth
The fourth animal at the zoo is the lion
None
```

One thing that you must keep in your mind is that you must define your inputs by putting them in commas like 'lion' or "lion" otherwise Python will throw an exception all the way along your coding process that the list or value is not defined. Putting the item in commas will help Python to define it properly.

127

Access by Index

You can access an individual item on the list by its **index**. An index is like an address that identifies the item's place in the list. The index appears directly after the list name, in between brackets, like this: list_name[index].

List indices begin with 0, not 1! You access the first item in a list like this: list_name[0]. The second item in a list is at index 1:list_name[1]. Computer scientists love to start counting from zero.

Instruction:

Write a statement that prints the result of adding the second and fourth items of the list. Make sure to access the list by index!

See Figure below:

```
script.py

1  numbers = [5, 6, 7, 8]
2
3  print "Adding the numbers at indices 0 and 2..."
4  print numbers[0] + numbers[2]
5  print "Adding the numbers at indices 1 and 3..."
6  # Your code here!
7
```

Your code will go like this:

```
7  print numbers[1] + numbers[3]
```

It will add numbers like this:

```
Adding the numbers at indices 0 and 2...
12
Adding the numbers at indices 1 and 3...
14
None
```

New Neighbors

A list index behaves like any other variable name! It can be used to access as well as assign values.

You saw how to access a list index like this:

```
zoo_animals[0]
# Gets the value "pangolin"
```

You can see how assignment works on line 5:

```
zoo_animals[2] = "hyena"
# Changes "sloth" to "hyena"
```

Instruction:

Write an assignment statement that will replace the item that currently holds the value "tiger" with another animal (as a string). It can be any animal you like.

See Figure below:

```
script.py

1  zoo_animals = ["pangolin", "cassowary", "sloth", "tiger"]
2  # Last night our zoo's sloth brutally attacked
3  #the poor tiger and ate it whole.
4
5  # The ferocious sloth has been replaced by a friendly hyena.
6  zoo_animals[2] = "hyena"
7
8  # What shall fill the void left by our dear departed tiger?
9  # Your code here!
10
```

The code will go like this:

```
10  zoo_animals[3]= "lion"
11  print zoo_animals
```

Late Arrivals & List Length

A list doesn't have to have a fixed length—you can add items to the end of a list any time you like! In Python, we say lists are **mutable**: that is, they can be changed.

You can add items to lists with the built-in list function `append()`, like this:

```
list_name.append(item)
```
Check it out: we've `append`ed a string to `suitcase` on line 2.

You can get the number of items in a list with the `len()` function (short for "length"), like so:

```
len(list_name)
```

One note before we begin. On the last line we are `print`ing `suitcase`. When this prints out, depending on your browser/OS configuration, you may notice a that the contents seem a little different. Each word might have a small `u` at the beginning. This is because, under the hood, strings in our version of Python are really `unicode` objects. You don't need to know anything about that, except that strings will have `type unicode` and that `"string" == u'string'` is `True`.

Instruction:

Append three more items to the suitcase list. (Maybe bring a bathing suit?) Then, set list_length equal to the length of suitcase.

See Figure below:

```
script.py

1  suitcase = []
2  suitcase.append("sunglasses")
3
4  # Your code here!
5
6
7
8
9  list_length = # Set this to the length of suitcase
10
11  print "There are %d items in the suitcase." % (list_length)
12  print suitcase
```

Your code will go like this:

```
5   suitcase.append("bathing suite")
6   suitcase.append("tooth brush")
7   suitcase.append("soap")
8
9   list_length = len(suitcase)
```

The whole code will seem like this:

```
script.py
1   suitcase = []
2   suitcase.append("sunglasses")
3
4   # Your code here!
5   suitcase.append("bathing suite")
6   suitcase.append("tooth brush")
7   suitcase.append("soap")
8
9   list_length = len(suitcase)
10
11  print "There are %d items in the suitcase." % (list_length)
12  print suitcase
```

This code will append the list of items in suitcase and specifying the list_length to the length of suitcase as len(suitcase) will print the items in suitcase like shown below:

```
There are 4 items in the suitcase.
['sunglasses', 'bathing suite', 'tooth brush', 'soap']
None
```

Now you could see the newly added items in your suitcase.

List Slicing

If you only want a small part of a list, that portion can be accessed using a special notation in the index brackets. `list_name[a:b]` will return a portion of `list_name` starting with the index a and ending *before* the index b.

If you tell Python `my_list = [0,1, 2, 3]`, then `my_list[1:3]` will return the list `[1, 2]`, leaving the original list unchanged! Check it out:

```
my_list = [0, 1, 2, 3]
my_slice = my_list[1:3]
print my_list
# Prints [0, 1, 2, 3]
print my_slice
# Prints [1, 2]
```

Instruction:

Use list slicing to make a list called first that's composed of just the first two items from suitcase, a list called middle containing only the two middle items from suitcase, and a list called last made up only of the last two items from suitcase. There are following items in suitcase:

```
1  suitcase = ["sunglasses", "hat", "passport", "laptop", "suit", "shoes"]
```

Your List Slicing Code will go like this:

```
3  first = suitcase [0:2]
4  middle = suitcase [2:4]
5  last = suitcase [4:6]
```

As you are thinking the way the Computer Scientists think, you must know that Computer Scientists love the digit 0 and therefore they love to start counting from 0. I will explain the code for you here as you will be little bit puzzled seeing the way code is written.

The first item will start from 0 instead of 1 and you are going to slice first two items so you will write it [0:2] instead of [1:2] and for next slicing pieces you will start from the last digit of your first code piece that is 2 and as laptop is 4th item in list, you will end with 4. It will be [2:4] instead of [3:4] and similar step for all other slices. As passport is 3rd item in list but the list starts from 0 so we will keep track of the way Computer Scientists think and also the way we think. So if you think your way the item will be 3 but as you start from 0 it will be 2.

Slicing Lists and Strings

You can slice a string exactly like a list! In fact, you can think of strings as lists of characters: each character is a sequential item in the list, starting from index 0.

If your list slice includes the very first or last item in a list (or a string), the index for that item doesn't have to be included. Here's an example:

my_list[:2]
Grabs the first two items

my_list[3:]
Grabs the fourth through last items

Instruction:

Assign each variable a slice of animals that spells out that variable's name. The animals for this purpose are these:

```
1   animals = "catdogfrog"
```

You will slice these animals like this:

```
2   cat = animals[:3]
3   dog = animals[3:6]
4   frog = animals[6:10]
```

Now I will explain the logic of slicing here. As described earlier the reason will be the same. If you are getting confused, you can write [:3] as [0:3] because Python will not mind it☺. Now as cat has three letters so it will end at 3 and dog will start from where cat ends i.e. 3 and will end at 6 as it has three letters too. So we will not disturb the logical sequence of counting in which we think and the sequence of counting that evolved due to the never ending love of Computer Scientists for digit 0.

Maintaining Order

You can search through a list with the `index()` function. `my_list.index("dog")` will return the first index that contains the string `"dog"`. An error will occur if there is no such item.

Items can be added to the middle of a list (instead of to the end) with the `insert()` function. `my_list.insert(4,"cat")` adds the item "cat" at index 4 of `my_list`, and moves the item previously at index 4 and all items following it to the next index (that is, they all get bumped towards the end by one).

Instruction:

Use the index() function to assign duck_index the index of the string equal to "duck". Then insert the string "cobra" at that index. See Figure below:

```
script.py
1  animals = ["aardvark", "badger", "duck", "emu", "fennec fox"]
2  duck_index =    # Use index() to find "duck"
3
4  # Your code here!
5
6
7
8  print animals # Observe what prints after the insert operation
```

Your code will go like this:

```
2  duck_index =    animals.index("duck")
3
4  animals.insert (duck_index, "cobra")
5
6
7
8  print animals
```

For One and All

If you want to do something with every item in the list, you can use a `for` loop. If you've learned about `for` loops in JavaScript, pay close attention! They're different in Python.

Here's the syntax:

```
for variable in list_name:
    # Do stuff!
```

A variable name follows the `for` keyword; it will be assigned the value of each list item in turn. In `list_name` designates `list_name` as the list the loop will work on. The line ends with a colon (`:`) and the indented code that follows it will be executed once per item in the list.

Instruction:

Write a statement in the indented part of the for loop that prints a number equal to 2 * number for every list item. Numbers we have used for this purpose are as shown below:

```
1  my_list = [1,9,3,8,5,7]
```

Your code will go like this:

```
3  for number in my_list:
4      print number * 2
```

The output of code will be the numbers multiplied by 2 like shown below:

```
2
18
6
16
10
14
None
```

More with 'for'

If your list is a jumbled mess, you may need to sort() it. my_list.sort() will sort the items in my_list in increasing numerical/alphabetical order.

It's worth noting that sort()does not return a *new* list; instead, your existing my_listis sorted **in place** (the sorted version replaces the unsorted version)

Instruction:

. Write a for loop that populates square_list with items that are the square (x ** 2) of each item in start_list. Then sort square_list!

See Figure below:

```
script.py

1   start_list = [5, 3, 1, 2, 4]
2   square_list = []
3
4   # Your code here!
5
6
7   print square_list
```

Your code will like this:

```
4   for x in start_list:
5       square_list.append(x**2)
6       square_list.sort()
7
8
9
10  print square_list
```

You will perform 2 functions here. You will denote the numbers in start_list with x and will append the square_list with x**2 so that it could sort the numbers that are square of other numbers. Sortng the square_list with .sort() will be the second function that will sort out square numbers from the list and will print those numbers to your console.

136

This Next Part is Key

A dictionary is similar to a list, but you access values by looking up a **key** instead of an index. A key can be any string or number. Dictionaries are enclosed in curly braces, like so:

```
d = {'key1' : 1, 'key2' : 2, 'key3' : 3}
```

This is a dictionary called d with three **key-value pairs**. The key 'key1' points to the value 1, 'key2' to 2, and so on.

Dictionaries are great for things like phone books (pairing a name with a phone number), login pages (pairing an e-mail address with a username), and more!

Instruction:

Print the values stored under the 'Sloth' and 'Burmese Python' keys. Accessing dictionary values by key is just like accessing list values by index:

```
residents['Puffin']
# Gets the value 104
```

See the Figure below:

```
script.py

1  # Assigning a dictionary with three key-value pairs to residents:
2  residents = {'Puffin' : 104, 'Sloth' : 105, 'Burmese Python' : 106}
3
4  print residents['Puffin'] # Prints Puffin's room number
5
6  # Your code here!
7
```

Your code to print keys and their values in residents will go like this:

```
6  print residents['Sloth']
7  print residents['Burmese Python']
```

New Entries

Like Lists, Dictionaries are "mutable". This means they can be changed after they are created. One advantage of this is that we can add new key/value pairs to the dictionary after it is created like so:

```
dict_name[new_key] = new_value
```

An empty pair of curly braces `{}` is an empty dictionary, just like an empty pair of `[]` is an empty list.

The length `len()` of a dictionary is the number of key-value pairs it has. Each pair counts only once, even if the value is a list. (That's right: you can put lists *inside* dictionaries!)

Instruction:

Add at least three more key-value pairs to the menu variable, with the dish name (as a "string") for the key and the price (a float or integer) as the value. Here's an example:

menu['Spam'] = 2.50

See Figure below:

```
script.py

1   menu = {} # Empty dictionary
2   menu['Chicken Alfredo'] = 14.50 # Adding new key-value pair
3   print menu['Chicken Alfredo']
4
5   # Your code here: Add some dish-price pairs to menu!
6
7
8
9
10  print "There are " + str(len(menu)) + " items on the menu."
11  print menu
```

Your code will go like this:

```
5    menu['Chicken Qorma']= 10.25
6    menu['Curry']= 15
7    menu['Pulses']= 20
```

Now your code will look like this:

```
script.py

1    menu = {} # Empty dictionary
2    menu['Chicken Alfredo'] = 14.50 # Adding new key-value pair
3    print menu['Chicken Alfredo']
4
5    menu['Chicken Qorma']= 10.25
6    menu['Curry']= 15
7    menu['Pulses']= 20
8
9
10   print "There are " + str(len(menu)) + " items on the menu."
11   print menu
```

Now with code you will be able to add items and their values to menu successfully as shown below:

```
14.5
There are 4 items on the menu.
{'Chicken Qorma': 10.25, 'Chicken Alfredo': 14.5, 'Pulses': 20, 'Curry': 15}
None
```

Changing Your Mind

Because dictionaries are mutable, they can be changed in many ways. Items can be removed from a dictionary with the `del` command:

```
del dict_name[key_name]
```

will remove the key `key_name`and its associated value from the dictionary.
A new value can be associated with a key by assigning a value to the key, like so:

```
dict_name[key] = new_value
```

Instruction

Delete the 'Sloth' and 'Bengal Tiger' items from zoo_animals using del.

Set the value associated with 'Rockhopper Penguin' to anything other than 'Arctic Exhibit'.

See Figure below:

```
script.py
1   # key - animal_name ; value - location
2   zoo_animals = { 'Unicorn' : 'Cotton Candy House',
3   'Sloth' : 'Rainforest Exhibit',
4   'Bengal Tiger' : 'Jungle House',
5   'Atlantic Puffin' : 'Arctic Exhibit',
6   'Rockhopper Penguin' : 'Arctic Exhibit'}
7   # A dictionary (or list) declaration may break across multiple lines
8
9   # Removing the 'Unicorn' entry. (Unicorns are incredibly expensive.)
10  del zoo_animals['Unicorn']
11
12  # Your code here!
13
14
15
16
17  print zoo_animals
```

Your code will go like this:

```
12   del zoo_animals['Sloth']
13   del zoo_animals['Bengal Tiger']
14   zoo_animals['Rockhopper Penguin']= "Quale"
```

The whole code will look like this:

```
script.py
1    # key - animal_name : value - location
2    zoo_animals = { 'Unicorn' : 'Cotton Candy House',
3    'Sloth' : 'Rainforest Exhibit',
4    'Bengal Tiger' : 'Jungle House',
5    'Atlantic Puffin' : 'Arctic Exhibit',
6    'Rockhopper Penguin' : 'Arctic Exhibit'}
7    # A dictionary (or list) declaration may break across multiple lines
8
9    # Removing the 'Unicorn' entry. (Unicorns are incredibly expensive.)
10   del zoo_animals['Unicorn']
11
12   del zoo_animals['Sloth']
13   del zoo_animals['Bengal Tiger']
14   zoo_animals['Rockhopper Penguin']= "Quale"
15
16
17   print zoo_animals
```

Now you will be able to make changes to zoo_animals by deleting and replacing the animals in list. The result will be like this:

```
{'Atlantic Puffin': 'Arctic Exhibit', 'Rockhopper Penguin': 'Quale'}
None
```

It's Dangerous to Go Alone! Take This

Let's go over a few last notes about **dictionaries**

1. A single dictionary can hold many types of values. The `inventory dict` here has both `int` and `list` values.

2. A dictionary's keys **MUST** be both immutable and hashable. Don't worry if you don't understand what that means. In general, we only use strings, numbers or tuples as keys, but not lists, dictionaries or sets. The values can be anything you'd like.

3. When you access a value in a dictionary you have access to that value directly. So if we have something like:

```
my_dict = {"hello":["h","e","l","l","o"]}
```

we can write `my_dict["hello"][1]` and the result will be `"e"`.

And one new thing about lists. Lists have a method called `.remove(VALUE)` which will remove the first instance of the value passed to it. For example:

```
beatles = ["john","paul","george","ringo","stuart"]
beatles.remove("stuart")
print beatles
>> ["john","paul","george","ringo"]
```

Now let's get some practice with dictionaries.

Instruction:

Final challenge! Add code that modifies the dictionary inventory in the following ways:

1. Add a key to inventory called 'pocket'
2. Set the value of 'pocket' to be a list consisting of the strings 'seashell', 'strange berry', and 'lint'
3. .sort() the items in the list stored under the 'backpack' key
4. Remove 'dagger' from the list of items stored under the 'backpack' key
5. Add 50 to the number stored under the 'gold' key

See the Figure below:

```
script.py

1   inventory = {'gold' : 500,
2   'pouch' : ['flint', 'twine', 'gemstone'], # Assigned a new list to 'pouch' key
3   'backpack' : ['xylophone','dagger', 'bedroll','bread loaf']}
4
5   # Adding a key 'burlap bag' and assigning a list to it
6   inventory['burlap bag'] = ['apple', 'small ruby', 'three-toed sloth']
7
8   # Sorting the list found under the key 'pouch'
9   inventory['pouch'].sort()
10  # Here the dictionary access expression takes the place of a list name
11
12  # Your code here
13
```

Your code will be something like this:

```
12   inventory['pocket'] = ['seashell', 'strange berry', 'lint']
13   inventory['backpack'].sort()
14   inventory['backpack'].remove('dagger')
15   inventory['gold'] = inventory['gold'] + 50
16   print inventory
```

Now with this code you will be able to add, sort and remove items and to alter the value of inventory item as well. The code will return the amended inventory list as shown below:

```
['pocket': ['seashell', 'strange berry', 'lint'], 'backpack': ['bedroll', 'bread loaf',
'xylophone'], 'pouch': ['flint', 'gemstone', 'twine'], 'burlap bag': ['apple', 'small
ruby', 'three-toed sloth'], 'gold': 550}
None
```

Hope you could have mastered not only the core techniques of Python so far but also the value of writing your code in small pieces with validation for every step and that's the reason that Python is considered as a language with low Bug Risk. The longer the coding, bigger the chances of Bugs in it. Interpreter provides you an opportunity to directly execute your code at any stage so that you could remove errors and exceptions from it.

Tuples and Sequences

We saw that lists and strings have many common properties, e.g., indexing and slicing operations. They are two examples of *sequence* data types. Since Python is an evolving language, other sequence data types may be added. There is also another standard sequence data type: the *tuple*.

A tuple consists of a number of values separated by commas, for instance:

```
>>> t = 12345, 54321, 'hello!'
>>> t[0]
12345
>>> t
(12345, 54321, 'hello!')
>>> # Tuples may be nested:
... u = t, (1, 2, 3, 4, 5)
>>> u
((12345, 54321, 'hello!'), (1, 2, 3, 4, 5))
```

As you see, on output tuples are alway enclosed in parentheses, so that nested tuples are interpreted correctly; they may be input with or without surrounding parentheses, although often parentheses are necessary anyway (if the tuple is part of a larger expression).

Tuples have many uses, e.g., (x, y) coordinate pairs, employee records from a database, etc. Tuples, like strings, are immutable: it is not possible to assign to the individual items of a tuple (you can simulate much of the same effect with slicing and concatenation, though).

A special problem is the construction of tuples containing 0 or 1 items: the syntax has some extra quirks to accommodate these. Empty tuples are constructed by an empty pair of parentheses; a tuple with one item is constructed by following a value with a comma (it is not sufficient to enclose a single value in parentheses). Ugly, but effective. For example:

```
>>> empty = ()
>>> singleton = 'hello',    # <-- note trailing comma
>>> len(empty)
0
>>> len(singleton)
1
>>> singleton
('hello',)
```

The statement t = 12345, 54321, 'hello!' is an example of *tuple packing*: the values 12345, 54321 and 'hello!' are packed together in a tuple. The reverse operation is also possible, e.g.:

```
>>> x, y, z = t
```

This is called, appropriately enough, *tuple unpacking*. Tuple unpacking requires that the list of variables on the left has the same number of elements as the length of the tuple. Note that multiple assignment is really just a combination of tuple packing and tuple unpacking!

Occasionally, the corresponding operation on lists is useful: *list unpacking*. This is supported by enclosing the list of variables in square brackets:

```
>>> a = ['spam', 'eggs', 100, 1234]
>>> [a1, a2, a3, a4] = a
```

DAY-10

MORE ON PYTHON FUNCTIONS

As you already know that function is a piece of code in a program. The function performs a specific task. The advantages of using functions are:

- Reducing duplication of code
- Decomposing complex problems into simpler pieces
- Improving clarity of the code
- Reuse of code
- Information hiding

Functions in Python are first-class citizens. It means that functions have equal status with other objects in Python. Functions can be assigned to variables, stored in collections or passed as arguments. This brings additional flexibility to the language.

There are two basic types of functions. Built-in functions and user defined ones. The built-in functions are part of the Python language. Examples are: dir(), len() or abs(). The user defined functions are functions created with the def keyword.

Creating a Function:

A function is created with the def keyword. The statements in the block of the function must be indented.

```
def function():
    pass
```

The def keyword is followed by the function name with round brackets and a colon. The indented statements form a *body* of the function.

The function is later executed when needed. We say that we *call* the function. If we call a function, the statements inside the function body are executed. They are not executed until the function is called.

```
myfunc()
```

To call a function, we specify the function name with the round brackets.

```
#!/usr/bin/python

"""
The ret.py script shows how to work with
functions in Python.
author: Jan Bodnar
ZetCode, 2011
"""


def showModuleName():
    print __doc__

def getModuleFile():
    return __file__

a = showModuleName()
b = getModuleFile()

print a, b
```

The string at the top of the script is called the documentation string. It documents the current script. The file in which we put Python code is called a *module*. We define two functions. The first function will print the module doc string. The second will return the path of our module. Function may or may not return a value. If they explicitly do not return a value, they implicitly returnNone. The __doc__ and __file__ are special state attributes. Note, that there are two underscores on both sides of the attribute.

```
$ ./ret.py
```

```
The ret.py script shows how to work with
functions in Python.
author: Jan Bodnar
ZetCode, 2011
```

```
None ./ret.py
```

Definitions of functions must precede their usage. Otherwise the interpreter will complain with aNameError.

```
#!/usr/bin/python

def f1():
    print "f1()"

f1()
#f2()

def f2():
    print "f2()"
```

In the above example we have two definitions of functions. One line is commented. Function call cannot be ahead of its definition.

```
#f2()

def f2():
    print "f2()"
```

We can call the f2() only after its definition. Uncommenting the line we get a NameError.

Where to define functions

Functions can be defined inside a module, a class or another function. Function defined inside a class is called a *method*.

```
#!/usr/bin/python

class Some:

    @staticmethod
    def f():
        print "f() method"

def f():
    print "f() function"

def g():
    def f():
```

148

```
        print "f() inner function"
    f()

Some.f()
f()
g()
```

In this example, we define an f() function in all possible places.

```
class Some:

    @staticmethod
    def f():
        print "f() method"
```

A static method is defined with a decorator in a Some class.

```
def f():
    print "f() function"
```

The function is defined in a module.

```
def g():
    def f():
        print "f() inner function"
    f()
```

Here the f() function is defined inside another g() function. It is an inner function.

```
Some.f()
f()
g()
```

The static method is called by specifying the class name, the dot operator and the function name with square brackets. Other functions are called using their names and square brackets.

```
$ ./defining.py
f() method
f() function
f() inner function
```

Output.

Functions are objects

Functions in Python are objects. They can be manipulated like other objects in Python. Therefore functions are called first-class citizens. This is not true in other OOP languages like Java or C#.

```
#!/usr/bin/python

def f():
    """This function prints a message """
    print "Today it is a cloudy day"

print isinstance(f, object)
print id(f)

print f.func_doc
print f.func_name
```

In this script we show, that our function is an object too.

```
def f():
    """This function prints a message """
    print "Today it is a cloudy day"
```

We define an f() function. It prints a message to the console. It has a documentation string.

```
print isinstance(f, object)
```

The isinstance() function checks, if the f() function is an instance of the object. All objects in Python inherit from this base entity.

```
print id(f)
```

Each object in Python has a unique id. The id() function returns the object's id.

```
print f.func_doc
print f.func_name
```

Objects may have attributes. Here we print two attributes of the function.

```
$ ./fobj.py
True
3077407212
This function prints a message
f
```

Output.

Objects can be stored in collections and passed to functions.

```
#!/usr/bin/python

def f():
    pass

def g():
    pass

def h(f):
    print id(f)

a = (f, g, h)

for i in a:
    print i

h(f)
h(g)
```

We define three functions. We place them in a tuple and pass them to a function.

```
a = (f, g, h)

for i in a:
    print i
```

We place three function objects in a tuple and traverse it with a for loop.

```
h(f)
h(g)
```

We pass the f(), g() functions to the h() function.

151

```
$ ./fobj2.py
<function f at 0xb7664fb4>
<function g at 0xb766c1b4>
<function h at 0xb766c3ac>
3076935604
3076964788
```

Output of the fobj.py script.

Three kinds of functions

Looking from a particular point of view, we can discern three kinds of functions. Functions that are always available for usage, functions that are contained within external modules, which must be imported and functions defined by a programmer with the def keyword.

```
#!/usr/bin/python

from math import sqrt

def cube(x):
    return x * x * x

print abs(-1)
print cube(9)
print sqrt(81)
```

Three kinds of functions are present in the above code.

```
from math import sqrt
```

The sqrt() function is imported from the math module.

```
def cube(x):
    return x * x * x
```

The cube() function is a custom defined function.

```
print abs(-1)
```

The abs() function is a built-in function readily accessible. It is part of the core of the language.

The return keyword

A function is created to do a specific task. Often there is a result from such a task. The returnkeyword is used to return values from a function. A function may or may not return a value. If a function does not have a return keyword, it will send a None value.

```
#!/usr/bin/python

def showMessage(msg):
    print msg

def cube(x):
    return x * x * x

x = cube(3)
print x

showMessage("Computation finished.")
print showMessage("Ready.")
```

We have two functions defined. One uses the return keyword, one does not.

```
def showMessage(msg):
    print msg
```

The showMessage() function does not return explicitly a value. It shows a message on the console.

```
def cube(x):
    return x * x * x
```

The cube() functions computes an expression and returns its result with the return keyword.

```
x = cube(3)
```

In this line we call the cube() function. The result of the computation of the cube() function is returned and assigned to the x variable. It holds the result value now.

```
showMessage("Computation finished.")
```

We call the showMessage() function with a message as a parameter. The message is printed to the console. We do not expect a value from this function.

```
print showMessage("Ready.")
```

This code produces two lines. One is a message printed by the showMessage() function. The other is the None value, which is implicitly sent by functions without the return statement.

```
$ ./return.py
27
Computation finished.
Ready.
None
```

Example output.

We can send more that one value from a function. The objects after the return keyword are separated by commas.

```
#!/usr/bin/python

n = [1, 2, 3, 4, 5]

def stats(x):
    mx = max(x)
    mn = min(x)
    ln = len(x)
    sm = sum(x)

    return mx, mn, ln, sm

mx, mn, ln, sm = stats(n)
print stats(n)

print mx, mn, ln, sm
```

There is a definition of a stats() function. This function returns four values.

154

```
return mx, mn, ln, sm
```

The return keyword sends back four numbers. The numbers are separated by a comma character. In fact, we have sent a tuple containing these four values. We could also return a list instead of a tuple.

```
mx, mn, ln, sm = stats(n)
```

The returned values are assigned to local variables.

```
$ ./return2.py
(5, 1, 5, 15)
5 1 5 15
```

Output.

Function redefinition

Python is dynamic in nature. It is possible to redefine an already defined function.

```
#!/usr/bin/python

from time import gmtime, strftime

def showMessage(msg):
    print msg

showMessage("Ready.")

def showMessage(msg):
    print strftime("%H:%M:%S", gmtime()),
    print msg

showMessage("Processing.")
```

We define a showMessage() function. Later we provide a new definition of the same function.

```
from time import gmtime, strftime
```

155

From the time module we import two functions which are used to compute the current time.

```
def showMessage(msg):
    print msg
```

This is the first definition of a function. It only prints a message to the console.

```
def showMessage(msg):
    print strftime("%H:%M:%S", gmtime()),
    print msg
```

Later in the source code, we set up a new definition of the showMessage() function. The message is preceded with a timestamp.

```
$ ./redefinition.py
Ready.
23:49:33 Processing.
```

Ouput of the script.

Function arguments

Most functions accept arguments. Arguments are values, that are sent to the function. The functions process the values and optionally return some value back.

```
#!/usr/bin/python

def C2F(c):
    return c * 9/5 + 32

print C2F(100)
print C2F(0)
print C2F(30)
```

In our example, we convert Celsius temperature to Fahrenheit. The C2F function accepts one argument c, which is the Celsius temperature.

```
$ ./fahrenheit.py
212
```

32
86

The arguments in Python functions may have implicit values. An implicit value is used, if no value is provided.

```
#!/usr/bin/python

def power(x, y=2):
    r = 1
    for i in range(y):
        r = r * x
    return r

print power(3)
print power(3, 3)
print power(5, 5)
```

Here we created a power function. The function has one argument with an implicit value. We can call the function with one or two arguments.

```
$ ./power.py
9
27
3125
```

Python functions can specify their arguments with a keyword. This means, that when calling a function, we specify both a keyword and a value. When we have multiple arguments and they are used without keywords, the order in which we pass those arguments is crucial. If we expect a name, age, sex in a function without keywords, we cannot change their order. If we use keywords, we can.

```
#!/usr/bin/python

def display(name, age, sex):
    print "Name: ", name
    print "Age: ", age
```

```
    print "Sex: ", sex

display("Lary", 43, "M")
display("Joan", 24, "F")
```

In this example, the order in which we specify the arguments is important. Otherwise, we get incorrect results.

```
$ ./persons.py
Name:  Lary
Age:  43
Sex:  M
Name:  Joan
Age:  24
Sex:  F
```

```
#!/usr/bin/python

# person2.py

def display(name, age, sex):
   print "Name: ", name
   print "Age: ", age
   print "Sex: ", sex

display(age=43, name="Lary", sex="M")
display(name="Joan", age=24, sex="F")
```

Now we call the functions with their keywords. The order may be changed, although it is not recommended to do so. Note, that we cannot use a non-keyword argument after a keyword argument. This would end in a syntax error.

```
display("Joan", sex="F", age=24)
```

This is a legal construct. A non-keyword argument may be followed by keyword arguments.

display(age=24, name="Joan", "F")

This will end in a syntax error. A non-keyword argument may not follow keyword arguments.

Functions in Python can even accept arbitrary number of arguments.

```
#!/usr/bin/python

def sum(*args):
   '''Function returns the sum
   of all values'''
   r = 0
   for i in args:
     r += i
   return r

print sum.__doc__
print sum(1, 2, 3)
print sum(1, 2, 3, 4, 5)
```

We use the * operator to indicate, that the function will accept arbitrary number of arguments. The sum() function will return the sum of all arguments. The first string in the function body is called the function documentation string. It is used to document the function. The string must be in triple quotes.

```
$ ./summation.py
Function returns the sum
   of all values
6
15
```

We can also use the ** construct in our functions. In such a case, the function will accept a dictionary. The dictionary has arbitrary length. We can then normally parse the dictionary, as usual.

```
#!/usr/bin/python

def display(**details):
```

```
for i in details:
    print "%s: %s" % (i, details[i])

display(name="Lary", age=43, sex="M")
```

This example demonstrates such a case. We can provide arbitrary number of key-value arguments. The function will handle them all.

```
$ ./person.py
age: 43
name: Lary
sex: M
```

Passing by reference

Parameters to functions are passed by reference. Some languages pass copies of the objects to functions. Passing objects by reference has two important conclusions. The process is faster than if copies of objects were passed. Mutable objects that are modified in functions are permanently changed.

```
#!/usr/bin/python

n = [1, 2, 3, 4, 5]

print "Original list:", n

def f(x):
    x.pop()
    x.pop()
    x.insert(0, 0)
    print "Inside f():", x

f(n)

print "After function call:", n
```

In our example, we pass a list of integers to a function. The object is modified inside the body of the function. After calling the function, the original object, the list of integers is modified.

```
def f(x):
    x.pop()
    x.pop()
    x.insert(0, 0)
    print "Inside f():", x
```

In the body of the function we work with the original object. Not with a copy of the object. In many programming languages we woud receive a copy of an object by default.

```
$ ./byreference.py
Original list: [1, 2, 3, 4, 5]
Inside f(): [0, 1, 2, 3]
After function call: [0, 1, 2, 3]
```

Global and local variables

Next we will talk about how variables are used in Python functions.

```
#!/usr/bin/python

name = "Jack"

def f():
    name = "Robert"
    print "Within function", name

print "Outside function", name
f()
```

A variable defined in a function body has a *local* scope. It is valid only within the body of the function.

```
$ ./local.py
Outside function Jack
```

161

Within function Robert

Output.

```
#!/usr/bin/python

name = "Jack"

def f():
  print "Within function", name

print "Outside function", name
f()
```

By default, we can get the contents of a *global* variable inside the body of a function. But if we want to change a global variable in a function, we must use the global keyword.

$ ./global.py
Outside function Jack
Within function Jack

```
#!/usr/bin/python

name = "Jack"

def f():
  global name
  name = "Robert"
  print "Within function", name

print "Outside function", name
f()
print "Outside function", name
```

Now, we will change the contents of a global name variable inside a function.

```
global name
name = "Robert"
```

Using the global keyword, we reference the variable defined outside the body of the function. The variable is given a new value.

```
$ ./global2.py
Outside function Jack
Within function Robert
Outside function Robert
```

Anonymous functions

It is possible to create anonymous functions in Python. Anonymous functions do not have a name. With the lambda keyword, little anonymous functions can be created. Anonymous functions are also called lambda functions by Python programmers. They are part of the functional paradigm incorporated in Python.

Lambda functions are restricted to a single expression. They can be used wherever normal functions can be used.

```
#!/usr/bin/python

y = 6

z = lambda x: x * y
print z(8)
```

This is a small example of the lambda function.

```
z = lambda x: x * y
```

The lambda keyword creates an anonymous function. The x is a parameter, that is passed to the lambda function. The parameter is followed by a colon character. The code next to the colon is the expression that is executed, when the lambda function is called. The lambda function is assigned to the z variable.

```
print z(8)
```

The lambda function is executed. The number 8 is passed to the anonymous function and it returns 48 as the result. Note that z is not a name for this function. It is only a variable to which the anonymous function was assigned.

```
$ ./lambda.py
48
```

Output of the example.

The lambda function can be used elegantly with other functional parts of the Python language, likemap() or filter() functions.

```
#!/usr/bin/python

cs = [-10, 0, 15, 30, 40]

ft = map(lambda t: (9.0/5)*t + 32, cs)
print ft
```

In the example we have a list of celsius temperatures. We create a new list containing temperatures in fahrenheit.

```
ft = map(lambda t: (9.0/5)*t + 32, cs)
```

The map() function applies the anonymous function to each element of the cs list. It creates a new ft list containing the computed fahrenheit temperatures.

```
$ ./lambda2.py
[14.0, 32.0, 59.0, 86.0, 104.0]
```

TWELVE THINGS TO REMEMBER

1. Functions

Functions in Python are created with the def keyword and take a name and an optional list of parameters. They can return values with the return keyword. Let's make and call the simplest possible function:

```
>>> def foo():
...     return 1
>>> foo()
1
```

The body of the function (as with all multi-line statements in Python) is mandatory and indicated by indentation. We can call functions by appending parentheses to the function name.

2. Scope

In Python functions create a new scope. Pythonistas might also say that functions have their own namespace. This means Python looks first in the namespace of the function to find variable names when it encounters them in the function body. Python includes a couple of functions that let us look at our namespaces. Let's write a simple function to investigate the difference between local and global scope.

```
>>> a_string = "This is a global variable"
>>> def foo():
...     print locals()
>>> print globals() # doctest: +ELLIPSIS
{..., 'a_string': 'This is a global variable'}
>>> foo() # 2
{}
```

The builtin globals function returns a dictionary containing all the variable names Python knows about. (For the sake of clarity I've omitted in the output a few variables Python automatically creates.) At point #2 I called my function foo which prints the contents of the local namespace inside the function. As we can see the function foo has its own separate namespace which is currently empty.

3. variable resolution rules

Of course this doesn't mean that we can't access global variables inside our function. Python's scope rule is that variable creation always creates a new local variable but variable access (including modification) looks in the local scope and then searches all the enclosing scopes to find a match. So if we modify our function footo print our global variable things work as we would expect:

```
>>> a_string = "This is a global variable"
>>> def foo():
...     print a_string # 1
>>> foo()
This is a global variable
```

At point #1 Python looks for a local variable in our function and not finding one, looks for a global variable[2] of the same name.

On the other hand if we try to assign to the global variable inside our function it doesn't do what we want:

```
>>> a_string = "This is a global variable"
>>> def foo():
...     a_string = "test" # 1
...     print locals()
>>> foo()
{'a_string': 'test'}
>>> a_string # 2
'This is a global variable'
```

As we can see, global variables can be accessed (even changed if they are mutable data types) but not (by default) assigned to. At point #1 inside our function we are actually creating a new local variable that "shadows" the global variable with the same name. We can see this be by printing the local namespace inside our function foo and notice it now has an entry. We can also see back out in the global namespace at point #2 that when we check the value of the variable a_string it hasn't been changed at all.

166

4. Variable lifetime

It's also important to note that not only do variables live inside a namespace, they also have lifetimes. Consider

```
>>> def foo():
...    x = 1
>>> foo()
>>> print x # 1
Traceback (most recent call last):
    ...
NameError: name 'x' is not defined
```

It isn't just scope rules at point #1 that cause a problem (although that's why we have a NameError) it also has to do with how function calls are implemented in Python and many other languages. There isn't any syntax we can use to get the value of the variable x at this point - it literally doesn't exist! The namespace created for our function foo is created from scratch each time the function is called and it is destroyed when the function ends.

5. Function arguments and parameters

Python does allow us to pass arguments to functions. The parameter names become local variables in our function.

```
>>> def foo(x):
...    print locals()
>>> foo(1)
{'x': 1}
```

Python has a variety of ways to define function parameters and pass arguments to them. For the full skinny you'll want to see the Python documentation on defining functions. I'll give you the short version here: function parameters can be either **positional** parameters that are **mandatory** or named, **default value** parameters that are **optional**.

```
>>> def foo(x, y=0): # 1
...    return x - y
>>> foo(3, 1) # 2
2
>>> foo(3) # 3
```

```
3
>>> foo() # 4
Traceback (most recent call last):
  ...
TypeError: foo() takes at least 1 argument (0 given)
>>> foo(y=1, x=3) # 5
2
```

At point #1 we are defining a function that has a single positional parameter x and a single named parameter y. As we see at point #2 we can call this function passing arguments normally - the values are passed to the parameters of foo by position even though one is defined in the function definition as a named parameter. We can also call the function without passing any arguments at all for the named parameter as you can see at point #3 - Python uses the default value of 0 we declared if it doesn't receive a value for the named parameter y. Of course we can't leave out values for the first (mandatory, positional) parameter - point #4 demonstrates that this results in an exception.

All clear and straightforward? Now it gets slightly confusing - Python supports named arguments at function call time. Look at point #5 - here we are calling a function with two named arguments even though it was **defined** with one named and one positional parameter. Since we have names for our parameters the order we pass them in doesn't matter.

The opposite case is true of course. One of the parameters for our function is defined as a named parameter but we passed an argument to it by position - the call foo(3,1) at point #2 passes a 3 as the argument to our ordered parameter x and passes the second (an integer 1) to the second parameter even though it was defined as a named parameter.

Whoo! That feels like a lot of words to describe a pretty simple concept: function parameters can have names or positions. This means slightly different things depending on whether we're at function definition or function call time and we can use named arguments to functions defined only with positional parameters and vice-versa! Again - if that was all too rushed be sure to check out the the docs.

6. Nested functions

Python allows the creation of nested functions. This means we can declare functions inside of functions and all the scoping and lifetime rules still apply normally.

```
>>> def outer():
...    x = 1
...    def inner():
...       print x # 1
...    inner() # 2
...
>>> outer()
1
```

This looks a little more complicated, but it's still behaving in a pretty sensible manner. Consider what happens at point #1 - Python looks for a local variable named x, failing it then looks in the enclosing scope which is another function! The variable x is a local variable to our function outer but as before our function inner has access to the enclosing scope (read and modify access at least). At point #2 we call our inner function. It's important to remember that inner is also just a variable name that follows Python's variable lookup rules - Python looks in the scope of outer first and finds a local variable named inner.

7. Functions are first class objects in Python

This is simply the observation that in Python, functions are objects like everything else. Ah, function containing variable, you're not so special!

```
>>> issubclass(int, object) # all objects in Python inherit from a common baseclass
True
>>> def foo():
...    pass
>>> foo.__class__ # 1
<type 'function'>
>>> issubclass(foo.__class__, object)
True
```

You may never have thought of your functions as having attributes - but functions are objects in Python, just like everything else. (If you find that confusing wait till you hear that classes are objects in Python, just like everything else!) Perhaps this is making the point in an academic way - functions are just regular values like any other kind of value in Python. That means you can pass functions to functions as arguments or return functions from functions as return values! If you've never thought of this sort of thing consider the following perfectly legal Python:

169

```
>>> def add(x, y):
...     return x + y
>>> def sub(x, y):
...     return x - y
>>> def apply(func, x, y): # 1
...     return func(x, y) # 2
>>> apply(add, 2, 1) # 3
3
>>> apply(sub, 2, 1)
1
```

This example might not seem too strange too you - add and sub are normal Python functions that receive two values and return a calculated value. At point #1 you can see that the variable intended to receive a function is just a normal variable like any other. At point #2 we are calling the function passed into apply - parentheses in Python are the call operator and call the value the variable name contains. And at point #3 you can see that passing functions as values doesn't have any special syntax in Python - function names are just variable labels like any other variable.

You might have seen this sort of behavior before - Python uses functions as arguments for frequently used operations like customizing the sorted builtin by providing a function to the key parameter. But what about returning functions as values? Consider:

```
>>> def outer():
...     def inner():
...         print "Inside inner"
...     return inner # 1
...
>>> foo = outer() #2
>>> foo # doctest:+ELLIPSIS
<function inner at 0x...>
>>> foo()
Inside inner
```

This may seem a little more bizarre. At point #1 I return the variable inner which happens to be a function label. There's no special syntax here - our function is returning the inner function which otherwise couldn't be called. Remember variable lifetime? The

170

function inner is freshly redefined each time the function outer is called but if inner wasn't returned from the function it would simply cease to exist when it went out of scope.

At point #2 we can catch the return value which is our function inner and store it in a new variable foo. We can see that if we evaluate foo it really does contain our function inner and we can call it by using the call operator (parentheses, remember?) This may look a little weird, but nothing to hard to understand so far, right? Hold on, because things are about to take a turn for the weird!

8. Closures

Let's not start with a definition, let's start with another code sample. What if we tweaked our last example slightly:

```
>>> def outer():
...     x = 1
...     def inner():
...         print x # 1
...     return inner
>>> foo = outer()
>>> foo.func_closure # doctest: +ELLIPSIS
(<cell at 0x...: int object at 0x...>,)
```

From our last example we can see that inner is a function returned by outer, stored in a variable named fooand we could call it with foo(). But will it run? Let's consider scoping rules first.

Everything works according to Python's scoping rules - x is a local variable in our function outer. Wheninner prints x at point #1 Python looks for a local variable to inner and not finding it looks in the enclosing scope which is the function outer, finding it there.

But what about things from the point of view of variable lifetime? Our variable x is local to the functionouter which means it only exists while the function outer is running. We aren't able to call inner till after the return of outer so according to our model of how Python works, x shouldn't exist anymore by the time we call inner and perhaps a runtime error of some kind should occur.

171

It turns out that, against our expectations, our returned inner function does work. Python supports a feature called **function closures** which means that inner functions defined in non-global scope remember what their enclosing namespaces looked like **at definition time**. This can be seen by looking at thefunc_closure attribute of our inner function which contains the variables in the enclosing scopes.

Remember - the function inner is being newly defined each time the function outer is called. Right now the value of x doesn't change so each inner function we get back does the same thing as another innerfunction - but what if we tweaked it a little bit?

```
>>> def outer(x):
...    def inner():
...       print x # 1
...    return inner
>>> print1 = outer(1)
>>> print2 = outer(2)
>>> print1()
1
>>> print2()
2
```

From this example you can see that **closures** - the fact that functions remember their enclosing scope - can be used to build custom functions that have, essentially, a hard coded argument. We aren't passing the numbers 1 or 2 to our inner function but are building custom versions of our inner function that "remembers" what number it should print.

This alone is a powerful technique - you might even think of it as similar to object oriented techniques in some ways: outer is a constructor for inner with x acting like a private member variable. And the uses are numerous - if you are familiar with the key parameter in Python's sorted function you have probably written a lambda function to sort a list of lists by the second item instead of the first. You might now be able to write an itemgetter function that accepts the index to retrieve and returns a function that could suitably be passed to the key parameter.

But let's not do anything so mundane with closures! Instead let's stretch one more time and write a decorator!

9. Decorators!

A decorator is just a callable that takes a function as an argument and returns a replacement function. We'll start simply and work our way up to useful decorators.

```
>>> def outer(some_func):
...     def inner():
...         print "before some_func"
...         ret = some_func() # 1
...         return ret + 1
...     return inner
>>> def foo():
...     return 1
>>> decorated = outer(foo) # 2
>>> decorated()
before some_func
2
```

Look carefully through our decorator example. We defined a function named outer that has a single parameter some_func. Inside outer we define an nested function named inner. The inner function will print a string then call some_func, catching its return value at point #1. The value of some_func might be different each time outer is called, but whatever function it is we'll call it. Finally inner returns the return value of some_func() + 1 - and we can see that when we call our returned function stored in decorated at point #2 we get the results of the print and also a return value of 2 instead of the original return value 1 we would expect to get by calling foo.

We could say that the variable decorated is a decorated version of foo - it's foo plus something. In fact if we wrote a useful decorator we might want to replace foo with the decorated version altogether so we always got our "plus something" version of foo. We can do that without learning any new syntax simply by re-assigning the variable that contains our function:

```
>>> foo = outer(foo)
>>> foo # doctest: +ELLIPSIS
<function inner at 0x...>
```

Now any calls to foo() won't get the original foo, they'll get our decorated version! Got the idea? Let's write a more useful decorator.

Imagine we have a library that gives us coordinate objects. Perhaps they are primarily made up of x and ycoordinate pairs. Sadly the coordinate objects don't support mathematical operators and we can't modify the source so we can't add this support ourselves. We're going to be doing a bunch of math, however, so we want to make add and sub functions that take two coordinate objects and do the appropriate mathematical thing. These functions would be easy to write (I'll provide a sample Coordinate class for the sake of illustration)

```
>>> class Coordinate(object):
...     def __init__(self, x, y):
...         self.x = x
...         self.y = y
...     def __repr__(self):
...         return "Coord: " + str(self.__dict__)
>>> def add(a, b):
...     return Coordinate(a.x + b.x, a.y + b.y)
>>> def sub(a, b):
...     return Coordinate(a.x - b.x, a.y - b.y)
>>> one = Coordinate(100, 200)
>>> two = Coordinate(300, 200)
>>> add(one, two)
Coord: {'y': 400, 'x': 400}
```

But what if our add and subtract functions had to also have some bounds checking behavior? Perhaps you can only sum or subtract based on positive coordinates and any result should be limited to positive coordinates as well. So currently

```
>>> one = Coordinate(100, 200)
>>> two = Coordinate(300, 200)
>>> three = Coordinate(-100, -100)
>>> sub(one, two)
Coord: {'y': 0, 'x': -200}
>>> add(one, three)
Coord: {'y': 100, 'x': 0}
```

but we'd rather have have the difference of one and two be {*x*: 0, *y*: 0} and the sum of one and three be {*x*: 100, *y*: 200} without modifying one, two, or three. Instead of adding bounds checking to the input arguments of each function and the return value of each function let's write a bounds checking decorator!

```
>>> def wrapper(func):
...     def checker(a, b): # 1
...         if a.x < 0 or a.y < 0:
...             a = Coordinate(a.x if a.x > 0 else 0, a.y if a.y > 0 else 0)
...         if b.x < 0 or b.y < 0:
...             b = Coordinate(b.x if b.x > 0 else 0, b.y if b.y > 0 else 0)
...         ret = func(a, b)
...         if ret.x < 0 or ret.y < 0:
...             ret = Coordinate(ret.x if ret.x > 0 else 0, ret.y if ret.y > 0 else 0)
...         return ret
...     return checker
>>> add = wrapper(add)
>>> sub = wrapper(sub)
>>> sub(one, two)
Coord: {'y': 0, 'x': 0}
>>> add(one, three)
Coord: {'y': 200, 'x': 100}
```

This decorator works just as before - returns a modified version of a function but in this case it does something useful by checking and normalizing the input parameters and the return value, substituting 0 for any negative x or y values.

It's a matter of opinion as to whether doing it this makes our code cleaner: isolating the bounds checking in its own function and applying it to all the functions we care to by wrapping them with a decorator. The alternative would be a function call on each input argument and on the resulting output before returning inside each math function and it is undeniable that using the decorator is at least less repetitious in terms of the amount of code needed to apply bounds checking to a function. In fact - if its our own functions we're decorating we could make the decorator application a little more obvious.

10. The @ symbol applies a decorator to a function

Python 2.4 provided support to wrap a function in a decorator by pre-pending the function definition with a decorator name and the @ symbol. In the code samples above we decorated our function by replacing the variable containing the function with a wrapped version.

```
>>> add = wrapper(add)
```

This pattern can be used at any time, to wrap any function. But if we are defining a function we can "decorate" it with the @ symbol like:

```
>>> @wrapper
... def add(a, b):
...     return Coordinate(a.x + b.x, a.y + b.y)
```

It's important to recognize that this is no different than simply replacing the original variable add with the return from the wrapper function - Python just adds some syntactic sugar to make what is going on very explicit.

Again - using decorators is easy! Even if writing useful decorators like staticmethod or classmethod would be difficult, using them is just a matter of prepending your function with @decoratorname!

11. *args and **kwargs

We've written a useful decorator but it's hard coded to work only on a particular kind of function - one which takes two arguments. Our inner function checker accepts two arguments and passes the arguments on to the function captured in the closure. What if we wanted a decorator that did something for any possible function? Let's write a decorator that increments a counter for every function call of every decorated function without changing any of it's decorated functions. This means it would have to accept the calling signature of any of the functions that it decorates and also call the functions it decorates passing on whatever arguments were passed to it.

It just so happens that Python has syntactic support for just this feature. Be sure to read the Python Tutorial for more details but the * operator used when defining a function means

176

that any extra positional arguments passed to the function end up in the variable prefaced with a *. So:

```
>>> def one(*args):
...     print args # 1
>>> one()
()
>>> one(1, 2, 3)
(1, 2, 3)
>>> def two(x, y, *args): # 2
...     print x, y, args
>>> two('a', 'b', 'c')
a b ('c',)
```

The first function one simply prints whatever (if any) positional arguments are passed to it. As you can see at point #1 we simply refer to the variable args inside the function - *args is only used in the function definition to indicate that positional arguments should be stored in the variable args. Python also allows us to specify some variables and catch any additional parameters in args as we can see at point #2.

The * operator can also be used when calling functions and here it means the analogous thing. A variable prefaced by * when **calling** a function means that the variable contents should be extracted and used as positional arguments. Again by example:

```
>>> def add(x, y):
...     return x + y
>>> lst = [1,2]
>>> add(lst[0], lst[1]) # 1
3
>>> add(*lst) # 2
3
```

The code at point #1 does exactly the same thing as the code at point #2 - Python is doing automatically for us at point #2 what we could do manually for ourselves. This isn't too bad - *args means either extract positional variables from an iterable if calling a function or when defining a function accept any extra positional variables.

Things get only slightly more complicated when we introduce ** which does for dictionaries & key/value pairs exactly what * does for iterables and positional parameters. Simple, right?

```
>>> def foo(**kwargs):
...    print kwargs
>>> foo()
{}
>>> foo(x=1, y=2)
{'y': 2, 'x': 1}
```

When we define a function we can use **kwargs to indicate that all uncaptured keyword arguments should be stored in a dictionary called kwargs. As before neither the name args nor kwargs is part of Python syntax but it is convention to use these variable names when declaring functions. Just like * we can use ** when calling a function as well as when defining it.

```
>>> dct = {'x': 1, 'y': 2}
>>> def bar(x, y):
...    return x + y
>>> bar(**dct)
3
```

12. More generic decorators

Given our new power we can write a decorator that "logs" the arguements to functions. We'll just print to stdout for simplicity sake:

```
>>> def logger(func):
...    def inner(*args, **kwargs): #1
...        print "Arguments were: %s, %s" % (args, kwargs)
...        return func(*args, **kwargs) #2
...    return inner
```

Notice our inner function takes any arbitrary number and type of parameters at point #1 and passes them along as arguments to the wrapped function at point #2. This allows us to wrap or decorate any function, no matter it's signature.

178

```
>>> @logger
... def foo1(x, y=1):
...     return x * y
>>> @logger
... def foo2():
...     return 2
>>> foo1(5, 4)
Arguments were: (5, 4), {}
20
>>> foo1(1)
Arguments were: (1,), {}
1
>>> foo2()
Arguments were: (), {}
2
```

PYTHON MAGIC METHODS

What are magic methods? They're everything in object-oriented Python. They're special methods that you can define to add "magic" to your classes. They're always surrounded by double underscores (e.g.__init__ or __lt__). They're also not as well documented as they need to be. All of the magic methods for Python appear in the same section in the Python docs, but they're scattered about and only loosely organized. There's hardly an example to be found in that section (and that may very well be by design, since they're all detailed in the *language reference*, along with boring syntax descriptions, etc.).

So, to fix what I perceived as a flaw in Python's documentation, I set out to provide some more plain-English, example-driven documentation for Python's magic methods. I started out with weekly blog posts, and now that I've finished with those, I've put together this guide.

I hope you enjoy it. Use it as a tutorial, a refresher, or a reference; it's just intended to be a user-friendly guide to Python's magic methods.

Construction and Initialization

Everyone knows the most basic magic method, __init__. It's the way that we can define the initialization behavior of an object. However, when I call x = SomeClass(), __init__ is not the first thing to get called. Actually, it's a method called __new__, which actually creates the instance, then passes any arguments at creation on to the initializer. At the other end of the object's lifespan, there's __del__. Let's take a closer look at these 3 magic methods:

__new__(cls, [...])
> __new__ is the first method to get called in an object's instantiation. It takes the class, then any other arguments that it will pass along to __init__. __new__ is used fairly rarely, but it does have its purposes, particularly when subclassing an immutable type like a tuple or a string. I don't want to go in to too much detail on __new__ because it's not too useful, but it is covered in great detail in the Python docs.

__init__(self, [...])
> The initializer for the class. It gets passed whatever the primary constructor was called with (so, for example, if we called x = SomeClass(10, 'foo'), __init__ would get passed 10 and 'foo' as arguments. __init__ is almost universally used in Python class definitions.

__del__(self)

> If __new__ and __init__ formed the constructor of the object, __del__ is the destructor. It doesn't implement behavior for the statement del x (so that code would not translate to x.__del__()). Rather, it defines behavior for when an object is garbage collected. It can be quite useful for objects that might require extra cleanup upon deletion, like sockets or file objects. Be careful, however, as there is no guarantee that __del__ will be executed if the object is still alive when the interpreter exits, so __del__ can't serve as a replacement for good coding practices (like always closing a connection when you're done with it. In fact, __del__ should almost never be used because of the precarious circumstances under which it is called; use it with caution!

Putting it all together, here's an example of __init__ and __del__ in action:

```python
from os.path import join

class FileObject:
    '''Wrapper for file objects to make sure the file gets closed on deletion.'''

    def __init__(self, filepath='~', filename='sample.txt'):
        # open a file filename in filepath in read and write mode
        self.file = open(join(filepath, filename), 'r+')

    def __del__(self):
        self.file.close()
        del self.file
```

Making Operators Work on Custom Classes

One of the biggest advantages of using Python's magic methods is that they provide a simple way to make objects behave like built-in types. That means you can avoid ugly, counter-intuitive, and nonstandard ways of performing basic operators. In some languages, it's common to do something like this:

```python
if instance.equals(other_instance):
    # do something
```

You could certainly do this in Python, too, but this adds confusion and is unnecessarily verbose. Different libraries might use different names for the same operations, making the client do way more work than necessary. With the power of magic methods, however, we can define one method (__eq__, in this case), and say what we *mean* instead:

```
if instance == other_instance:
    #do something
```

That's part of the power of magic methods. The vast majority of them allow us to define meaning for operators so that we can use them on our own classes just like they were built in types.

Comparison magic methods

Python has a whole slew of magic methods designed to implement intuitive comparisons between objects using operators, not awkward method calls. They also provide a way to override the default Python behavior for comparisons of objects (by reference). Here's the list of those methods and what they do:

__cmp__(self, other)
> __cmp__ is the most basic of the comparison magic methods. It actually implements behavior for all of the comparison operators (<, ==, !=, etc.), but it might not do it the way you want (for example, if whether one instance was equal to another were determined by one criterion and and whether an instance is greater than another were determined by something else). __cmp__ should return a negative integer if self < other, zero if self == other, and positive if self > other. It's usually best to define each comparison you need rather than define them all at once, but __cmp__ can be a good way to save repetition and improve clarity when you need all comparisons implemented with similar criteria.

__eq__(self, other)
> Defines behavior for the equality operator, ==.

__ne__(self, other)
> Defines behavior for the inequality operator, !=.

__lt__(self, other)
> Defines behavior for the less-than operator, <.

__gt__(self, other)
> Defines behavior for the greater-than operator, >.

__le__(self, other)
> Defines behavior for the less-than-or-equal-to operator, <=.

__ge__(self, other)
> Defines behavior for the greater-than-or-equal-to operator, >=.

For an example, consider a class to model a word. We might want to compare words lexicographically (by the alphabet), which is the default comparison behavior for strings, but we also might want to do it based on some other criterion, like length or number of syllables. In this example, we'll compare by length. Here's an implementation:

```python
class Word(str):
    '''Class for words, defining comparison based on word length.'''

    def __new__(cls, word):
        # Note that we have to use __new__. This is because str is an immutable
        # type, so we have to initialize it early (at creation)
        if ' ' in word:
            print "Value contains spaces. Truncating to first space."
            word = word[:word.index(' ')] # Word is now all chars before first space
        return str.__new__(cls, word)

    def __gt__(self, other):
        return len(self) > len(other)
    def __lt__(self, other):
        return len(self) < len(other)
    def __ge__(self, other):
        return len(self) >= len(other)
    def __le__(self, other):
        return len(self) <= len(other)
```

Now, we can create two Words (by using Word('foo') and Word('bar')) and compare them based on length. Note, however, that we didn't define __eq__ and __ne__. This is because this would lead to some weird behavior (notably that Word('foo') == Word('bar') would evaluate to true). It wouldn't make sense to test for equality based on length, so we fall back on str's implementation of equality.

Now would be a good time to note that you don't have to define every comparison magic method to get rich comparisons. The standard library has kindly provided us with a class decorator in the modulefunctools that will define all rich comparison methods if you only define __eq__ and one other (e.g.__gt__, __lt__, etc.) This feature is only available in Python 2.7, but when you get a chance it saves a great deal of time and effort. You can use it by placing @total_ordering above your class definition.

Numeric magic methods

Just like you can create ways for instances of your class to be compared with comparison operators, you can define behavior for numeric operators. Buckle your seat belts, folks, there's a lot of these. For organization's sake, I've split the numeric magic methods into 5 categories: unary operators, normal arithmetic operators, reflected arithmetic operators (more on this later), augmented assignment, and type conversions.

Unary operators and functions

Unary operators and functions only have one operand, e.g. negation, absolute value, etc.

__pos__(self)
> Implements behavior for unary positive (e.g. +some_object)

__neg__(self)
> Implements behavior for negation (e.g. -some_object)

__abs__(self)
> Implements behavior for the built in abs() function.

__invert__(self)
> Implements behavior for inversion using the ~ operator.

__round__(self, n)
> Implements behavior for the buil in round() function. n is the number of decimal places to round to.

__floor__(self)
> Implements behavior for math.floor(), i.e., rounding down to the nearest integer.

__ceil__(self)
> Implements behavior for math.ceil(), i.e., rounding up to the nearest integer.

__trunc__(self)

Implements behavior for math.trunc(), i.e., truncating to an integral.

Normal arithmetic operators

Now, we cover the typical binary operators (and a function or two): +, -, * and the like. These are, for the most part, pretty self-explanatory.

__add__(self, other)
    Implements addition.

__sub__(self, other)
    Implements subtraction.

__mul__(self, other)
    Implements multiplication.

__floordiv__(self, other)
    Implements integer division using the // operator.

__div__(self, other)
    Implements division using the / operator.

__truediv__(self, other)
    Implements *true* division. Note that this only works when from __future__ import division is in effect.

__mod__(self, other)
    Implements modulo using the % operator.

__divmod__(self, other)
    Implements behavior for long division using the divmod() built in function.

__pow__
    Implements behavior for exponents using the ** operator.

__lshift__(self, other)
    Implements left bitwise shift using the << operator.

__rshift__(self, other)
    Implements right bitwise shift using the >> operator.

__and__(self, other)
    Implements bitwise and using the & operator.

__or__(self, other)
>   Implements bitwise or using the | operator.

__xor__(self, other)
>   Implements bitwise xor using the ^ operator.

Reflected arithmetic operators

You know how I said I would get to reflected arithmetic in a bit? Some of you might think it's some big, scary, foreign concept. It's actually quite simple. Here's an example:

```
some_object + other
```

That was "normal" addition. The reflected equivalent is the same thing, except with the operands switched around:

```
other + some_object
```

So, all of these magic methods do the same thing as their normal equivalents, except the perform the operation with other as the first operand and self as the second, rather than the other way around. In most cases, the result of a reflected operation is the same as its normal equivalent, so you may just end up defining __radd__ as calling __add__ and so on. Note that the object on the left hand side of the operator (other in the example) must not define (or return NotImplemented) for its definition of the non-reflected version of an operation. For instance, in the example, some_object.__radd__ will only be called if otherdoes not define __add__.

__radd__(self, other)
>   Implements reflected addition.

__rsub__(self, other)
>   Implements reflected subtraction.

__rmul__(self, other)
>   Implements reflected multiplication.

__rfloordiv__(self, other)
>   Implements reflected integer division using the // operator.

186

__rdiv__(self, other)
>   Implements reflected division using the / operator.

__rtruediv__(self, other)
>   Implements reflected *true* division. Note that this only works when from __future__ import division is in effect.

__rmod__(self, other)
>   Implements reflected modulo using the % operator.

__rdivmod__(self, other)
>   Implements behavior for long division using the divmod() built in function, when divmod(other, self) is called.

__rpow__
>   Implements behavior for reflected exponents using the ** operator.

__rlshift__(self, other)
>   Implements reflected left bitwise shift using the << operator.

__rrshift__(self, other)
>   Implements reflected right bitwise shift using the >> operator.

__rand__(self, other)
>   Implements reflected bitwise and using the & operator.

__ror__(self, other)
>   Implements reflected bitwise or using the | operator.

__rxor__(self, other)
>   Implements reflected bitwise xor using the ^ operator.

Augmented assignment

Python also has a wide variety of magic methods to allow custom behavior to be defined for augmented assignment. You're probably already familiar with augmented assignment, it combines "normal" operators with assignment. If you still don't know what I'm talking about, here's an example:

```
x = 5
x += 1 # in other words x = x + 1
```

Each of these methods should return the value that the variable on the left hand side should be assigned to (for instance, for a += b, __iadd__ might return a + b, which would be assigned to a). Here's the list:

__iadd__(self, other)
> Implements addition with assignment.

__isub__(self, other)
> Implements subtraction with assignment.

__imul__(self, other)
> Implements multiplication with assignment.

__ifloordiv__(self, other)
> Implements integer division with assignment using the //= operator.

__idiv__(self, other)
> Implements division with assignment using the /= operator.

__itruediv__(self, other)
> Implements *true* division with assignment. Note that this only works when from __future__ import division is in effect.

__imod__(self, other)
> Implements modulo with assignment using the %= operator.

__ipow__
> Implements behavior for exponents with assignment using the **= operator.

__ilshift__(self, other)
> Implements left bitwise shift with assignment using the <<= operator.

__irshift__(self, other)
> Implements right bitwise shift with assignment using the >>= operator.

__iand__(self, other)
> Implements bitwise and with assignment using the &= operator.

__ior__(self, other)
> Implements bitwise or with assignment using the |= operator.

__ixor__(self, other)
> Implements bitwise xor with assignment using the ^= operator.

Type conversion magic methods

Python also has an array of magic methods designed to implement behavior for built in type conversion functions like float(). Here they are:

__int__(self)
> Implements type conversion to int.

__long__(self)
> Implements type conversion to long.

__float__(self)
> Implements type conversion to float.

__complex__(self)
> Implements type conversion to complex.

__oct__(self)
> Implements type conversion to octal.

__hex__(self)
> Implements type conversion to hexadecimal.

__index__(self)
> Implements type conversion to an int when the object is used in a slice expression. If you define a custom numeric type that might be used in slicing, you should define __index__.

__trunc__(self)
> Called when math.trunc(self) is called. __trunc__ should return the value of `self truncated to an integral type (usually a long).

__coerce__(self, other)
> Method to implement mixed mode arithmetic. __coerce__ should return None if type conversion is impossible. Otherwise, it should return a pair (2-tuple) of self and other, manipulated to have the same type.

Representing your Classes

It's often useful to have a string representation of a class. In Python, there's a few methods that you can implement in your class definition to customize how built in functions that return representations of your class behave.

__str__(self)

    Defines behavior for when str() is called on an instance of your class.

__repr__(self)

    Defines behavior for when repr() is called on an instance of your class. The major difference between str() and repr() is intended audience. repr() is intended to produce output that is mostly machine-readable (in many cases, it could be valid Python code even), whereas str() is intended to be human-readable.

__unicode__(self)

    Defines behavior for when unicode() is called on an instance of your class. unicode() is like str(), but it returns a unicode string. Be wary: if a client calls str() on an instance of your class and you've only defined __unicode__(), it won't work. You should always try to define __str__() as well in case someone doesn't have the luxury of using unicode.

__format__(self, formatstr)

    Defines behavior for when an instance of your class is used in new-style string formatting. For instance, "Hello, {0:abc}!".format(a) would lead to the call a.__format__("abc"). This can be useful for defining your own numerical or string types that you might like to give special formatting options.

__hash__(self)

    Defines behavior for when hash() is called on an instance of your class. It has to return an integer, and its result is used for quick key comparison in dictionaries. Note that this usually entails implementing __eq__ as well. Live by the following rule: a == b implies hash(a) == hash(b).

__nonzero__(self)

    Defines behavior for when bool() is called on an instance of your class. Should return True or False, depending on whether you would want to consider the instance to be True or False.

__dir__(self)

    Defines behavior for when dir() is called on an instance of your class. This method should return a list of attributes for the user. Typically, implementing __dir__ is unnecessary, but it can be vitally important for interactive use of your classes if you redefine __getattr__ or __getattribute__ (which you will see in the next section) or are otherwise dynamically generating attributes.

__sizeof__(self)

Defines behavior for when sys.getsizeof() is called on an instance of your class. This should return the size of your object, in bytes. This is generally more useful for Python classes implemented in C extensions, but it helps to be aware of it.

We're pretty much done with the boring (and example-free) part of the magic methods guide. Now that we've covered some of the more basic magic methods, it's time to move to more advanced material.

Controlling Attribute Access

Many people coming to Python from other languages complain that it lacks true encapsulation for classes (e.g. no way to define private attributes and then have public getter and setters). This couldn't be farther than the truth: it just happens that Python accomplishes a great deal of encapsulation through "magic", instead of explicit modifiers for methods or fields. Take a look:

__getattr__(self, name)
> You can define behavior for when a user attempts to access an attribute that doesn't exist (either at all or yet). This can be useful for catching and redirecting common misspellings, giving warnings about using deprecated attributes (you can still choose to compute and return that attribute, if you wish), or deftly handing an AttributeError. It only gets called when a nonexistent attribute is accessed, however, so it isn't a true encapsulation solution.

__setattr__(self, name, value)
> Unlike __getattr__, __setattr__ is an encapsulation solution. It allows you to define behavior for assignment to an attribute regardless of whether or not that attribute exists, meaning you can define custom rules for any changes in the values of attributes. However, you have to be careful with how you use __setattr__, as the example at the end of the list will show.

__delattr__
> This is the exact same as __setattr__, but for deleting attributes instead of setting them. The same precautions need to be taken as with __setattr__ as well in order to prevent infinite recursion (calling del self.name in the implementation of __delattr__ would cause infinite recursion).

__getattribute__(self, name)
> After all this, __getattribute__ fits in pretty well with its companions __setattr__ and __delattr__. However, I don't recommend you use

it. __getattribute__ can only be used with new-style classes (all classes are new-style in the newest versions of Python, and in older versions you can make a class new-style by subclassing object. It allows you to define rules for whenever an attribute's value is accessed. It suffers from some similar infinite recursion problems as its partners-in-crime (this time you call the base class's __getattribute__ method to prevent this). It also mainly obviates the need for __getattr__, which only gets called when __getattribute__ is implemented if it is called explicitly or an AttributeError is raised. This method can be used (after all, it's your choice), but I don't recommend it because it has a small use case (it's far more rare that we need special behavior to retrieve a value than to assign to it) and because it can be really difficult to implement bug-free.

You can easily cause a problem in your definitions of any of the methods controlling attribute access. Consider this example:

```python
def __setattr__(self, name, value):
    self.name = value
    # since every time an attribute is assigned, __setattr__() is called, this
    # is recursion.
    # so this really means self.__setattr__('name', value). Since the method
    # keeps calling itself, the recursion goes on forever causing a crash

def __setattr__(self, name, value):
    self.__dict__[name] = value # assigning to the dict of names in the class
    # define custom behavior here
```

Again, Python's magic methods are incredibly powerful, and with great power comes great responsibility. It's important to know the proper way to use magic methods so you don't break any code.

So, what have we learned about custom attribute access in Python? It's not to be used lightly. In fact, it tends to be excessively powerful and counter-intuitive. But the reason why it exists is to scratch a certain itch: Python doesn't seek to make bad things impossible, but just to make them difficult. Freedom is paramount, so you can really do whatever you want. Here's an example of some of the special attribute access methods in action (note that we use super because not all classes have an attribute __dict__):

```python
class AccessCounter(object):
    '''A class that contains a value and implements an access counter.
    The counter increments each time the value is changed.'''

    def __init__(self, val):
        super(AccessCounter, self).__setattr__('counter', 0)
        super(AccessCounter, self).__setattr__('value', val)

    def __setattr__(self, name, value):
        if name == 'value':
            super(AccessCounter, self).__setattr__('counter', self.counter + 1)
        # Make this unconditional.
        # If you want to prevent other attributes to be set, raise AttributeError(name)
        super(AccessCounter, self).__setattr__(name, value)

    def __delattr__(self, name):
        if name == 'value':
            super(AccessCounter, self).__setattr__('counter', self.counter + 1)
        super(AccessCounter, self).__delattr__(name)]
```

Making Custom Sequences

There's a number of ways to get your Python classes to act like built in sequences (dict, tuple, list, string, etc.). These are by far my favorite magic methods in Python because of the absurd degree of control they give you and the way that they magically make a whole array of global functions work beautifully on instances of your class. But before we get down to the good stuff, a quick word on requirements.

Requirements

Now that we're talking about creating your own sequences in Python, it's time to talk about *protocols*. Protocols are somewhat similar to interfaces in other languages in that they give you a set of methods you must define. However, in Python protocols are totally informal and require no explicit declarations to implement. Rather, they're more like guidelines.

Why are we talking about protocols now? Because implementing custom container types in Python involves using some of these protocols. First, there's the protocol for defining immutable containers: to make an immutable container, you need only define __len__ and __getitem__ (more on these later). The mutable container protocol requires everything that immutable containers require plus __setitem__ and__delitem__. Lastly, if you want your object to be iterable, you'll have to define __iter__, which returns an iterator. That iterator must conform to an iterator protocol, which requires iterators to have methods called __iter__(returning itself) and next.

The magic behind containers

Without any more wait, here are the magic methods that containers use:

__len__(self)
> Returns the length of the container. Part of the protocol for both immutable and mutable containers.

__getitem__(self, key)
> Defines behavior for when an item is accessed, using the notation self[key]. This is also part of both the mutable and immutable container protocols. It should also raise appropriate exceptions:TypeError if the type of the key is wrong and KeyError if there is no corresponding value for the key.

__setitem__(self, key, value)
> Defines behavior for when an item is assigned to, using the notation self[nkey] = value. This is part of the mutable container protocol. Again, you should raise KeyError and TypeError where appropriate.

__delitem__(self, key)
> Defines behavior for when an item is deleted (e.g. del self[key]). This is only part of the mutable container protocol. You must raise the appropriate exceptions when an invalid key is used.

__iter__(self)
> Should return an iterator for the container. Iterators are returned in a number of contexts, most notably by the iter() built in function and when a container is looped over using the form for x in container:. Iterators are their own objects, and they also must define an __iter__ method that returns self.

__reversed__(self)
> Called to implement behavior for the reversed() built in function. Should return a reversed version of the sequence. Implement this only if the sequence class is ordered, like list or tuple.

__contains__(self, item)

> __contains__ defines behavior for membership tests using in and not in. Why isn't this part of a sequence protocol, you ask? Because when __contains__ isn't defined, Python just iterates over the sequence and returns True if it comes across the item it's looking for.

__missing__(self, key)

> __missing__ is used in subclasses of dict. It defines behavior for whenever a key is accessed that does not exist in a dictionary (so, for instance, if I had a dictionary d and said d["george"] when"george" is not a key in the dict, d.__missing__("george") would be called).

An example

For our example, let's look at a list that implements some functional constructs that you might be used to from other languages (Haskell, for example).

```python
class FunctionalList:
    '''A class wrapping a list with some extra functional magic, like head,
    tail, init, last, drop, and take.'''

    def __init__(self, values=None):
        if values is None:
            self.values = []
        else:
            self.values = values

    def __len__(self):
        return len(self.values)

    def __getitem__(self, key):
        # if key is of invalid type or value, the list values will raise the error
        return self.values[key]

    def __setitem__(self, key, value):
        self.values[key] = value

    def __delitem__(self, key):
        del self.values[key]

    def __iter__(self):
```

```
        return iter(self.values)

    def __reversed__(self):
        return FunctionalList(reversed(self.values))

    def append(self, value):
        self.values.append(value)
    def head(self):
        # get the first element
        return self.values[0]
    def tail(self):
        # get all elements after the first
        return self.values[1:]
    def init(self):
        # get elements up to the last
        return self.values[:-1]
    def last(self):
        # get last element
        return self.values[-1]
    def drop(self, n):
        # get all elements except first n
        return self.values[n:]
    def take(self, n):
        # get first n elements
        return self.values[:n]
```

There you have it, a (marginally) useful example of how to implement your own sequence.
Of course, there are more useful applications of custom sequences, but quite a few of them
are already implemented in the standard library (batteries included, right?),
like Counter, OrderedDict, and NamedTuple.

Reflection

You can also control how reflection using the built in
functions isinstance() and issubclass()behaves by defining magic methods. The magic
methods are:

__instancecheck__(self, instance)
        Checks if an instance is an instance of the class you defined
        (e.g. isinstance(instance, class).

__subclasscheck__(self, subclass)
> Checks if a class subclasses the class you defined (e.g. issubclass(subclass, class)).

The use case for these magic methods might seem small, and that may very well be true. I won't spend too much more time on reflection magic methods because they aren't very important, but they reflect something important about object-oriented programming in Python and Python in general: there is almost always an easy way to do something, even if it's rarely necessary. These magic methods might not seem useful, but if you ever need them you'll be glad that they're there (and that you read this guide!).

Callable Objects

As you may already know, in Python, functions are first-class objects. This means that they can be passed to functions and methods just as if they were objects of any other kind. This is an incredibly powerful feature.

A special magic method in Python allows instances of your classes to behave as if they were functions, so that you can "call" them, pass them to functions that take functions as arguments, and so on. This is another powerful convenience feature that makes programming in Python that much sweeter.

__call__(self, [args...])
> Allows an instance of a class to be called as a function. Essentially, this means that x() is the same as x.__call__(). Note that __call__ takes a variable number of arguments; this means that you define __call__ as you would any other function, taking however many arguments you'd like it to.

__call__ can be particularly useful in classes whose instances that need to often change state. "Calling" the instance can be an intuitive and elegant way to change the object's state. An example might be a class representing an entity's position on a plane:

```python
class Entity:
    '''Class to represent an entity. Callable to update the entity's position.'''

    def __init__(self, size, x, y):
        self.x, self.y = x, y
        self.size = size
```

```
    def __call__(self, x, y):
        '''Change the position of the entity.'''
        self.x, self.y = x, y

    # snip...
```

Context Managers

In Python 2.5, a new keyword was introduced in Python along with a new method for code reuse, the with statement. The concept of context managers was hardly new in Python (it was implemented before as a part of the library), but not until __PEP 343__ was accepted did it achieve status as a first class language construct. You may have seen with statements before:

```
with open('foo.txt') as bar:
    # perform some action with bar
```

Context managers allow setup and cleanup actions to be taken for objects when their creation is wrapped with a with statement. The behavior of the context manager is determined by two magic methods:

__enter__(self)
> Defines what the context manager should do at the beginning of the block created by the withstatement. Note that the return value of __enter__ is bound to the *target* of the with statement, or the name after the as.

__exit__(self, exception_type, exception_value, traceback)
> Defines what the context manager should do after its block has been executed (or terminates). It can be used to handle exceptions, perform cleanup, or do something always done immediately after the action in the block. If the block executes successfully, exception_type, exception_value, and traceback will be None. Otherwise, you can choose to handle the exception or let the user handle it; if you want to handle it, make sure __exit__ returns True after all is said and done. If you don't want the exception to be handled by the context manager, just let it happen.

198

__enter__ and __exit__ can be useful for specific classes that have well-defined and common behavior for setup and cleanup. You can also use these methods to create generic context managers that wrap other objects. Here's an example:

```python
class Closer:
    '''A context manager to automatically close an object with a close method
    in a with statement.'''

    def __init__(self, obj):
        self.obj = obj

    def __enter__(self):
        return self.obj # bound to target

    def __exit__(self, exception_type, exception_val, trace):
        try:
            self.obj.close()
        except AttributeError: # obj isn't closable
            print 'Not closable.'
            return True # exception handled successfully
```

Here's an example of Closer in action, using an FTP connection to demonstrate it (a closable socket):

```python
>>> from magicmethods import Closer
>>> from ftplib import FTP
>>> with Closer(FTP('ftp.somesite.com')) as conn:
...     conn.dir()
...
# output omitted for brevity
>>> conn.dir()
# long AttributeError message, can't use a connection that's closed
>>> with Closer(int(5)) as i:
...     i += 1
...
Not closable.
>>> i
6
```

See how our wrapper gracefully handled both proper and improper uses? That's the power of context managers and magic methods. Note that the Python standard library includes a module <u>contextlib</u> that contains a context manager, contextlib.closing(), that does approximately the same thing (without any handling of the case where an object does not have a close() method).

Abstract Base Classes

See http://docs.python.org/2/library/abc.html.

Building Descriptor Objects

Descriptors are classes which, when accessed through either getting, setting, or deleting, can also alter other objects. Descriptors aren't meant to stand alone; rather, they're meant to be held by an owner class. Descriptors can be useful when building object-oriented databases or classes that have attributes whose values are dependent on each other. Descriptors are particularly useful when representing attributes in several different units of measurement or representing computed attributes (like distance from the origin in a class to represent a point on a grid).

To be a descriptor, a class must have at least one of __get__, __set__, and __delete__ implemented. Let's take a look at those magic methods:

__get__(self, instance, owner)
> Define behavior for when the descriptor's value is retrieved. instance is the instance of the owner object. owner is the owner class itself.

__set__(self, instance, value)
> Define behavior for when the descriptor's value is changed. instance is the instance of the owner class and value is the value to set the descriptor to.

__delete__(self, instance)
> Define behavior for when the descriptor's value is deleted. instance is the instance of the owner object.

Now, an example of a useful application of descriptors: unit conversions.

```python
class Meter(object):
    '''Descriptor for a meter.'''

    def __init__(self, value=0.0):
        self.value = float(value)
    def __get__(self, instance, owner):
        return self.value
    def __set__(self, instance, value):
        self.value = float(value)

class Foot(object):
    '''Descriptor for a foot.'''

    def __get__(self, instance, owner):
        return instance.meter * 3.2808
    def __set__(self, instance, value):
        instance.meter = float(value) / 3.2808

class Distance(object):
    '''Class to represent distance holding two descriptors for feet and
    meters.'''
    meter = Meter()
    foot = Foot()
```

Copying

Sometimes, particularly when dealing with mutable objects, you want to be able to copy an object and make changes without affecting what you copied from. This is where Python's copy comes into play. However (fortunately), Python modules are not sentient, so we don't have to worry about a Linux-based robot uprising, but we do have to tell Python how to efficiently copy things.

__copy__(self)
> Defines behavior for copy.copy() for instances of your class. copy.copy() returns a *shallow copy* of your object -- this means that, while the instance itself is a new instance, all of its data is referenced -- i.e., the object itself is copied, but its data is still referenced (and hence changes to data in a shallow copy may cause changes in the original).

__deepcopy__(self, memodict={})

201

Defines behavior for copy.deepcopy() for instances of your class. copy.deepcopy() returns a *deep copy* of your object -- the object *and* its data are both copied. memodict is a cache of previously copied objects -- this optimizes copying and prevents infinite recursion when copying recursive data structures. When you want to deep copy an individual attribute, call copy.deepcopy() on that attribute with memodict as the first argument.

What are some use cases for these magic methods? As always, in any case where you need more fine-grained control than what the default behavior gives you. For instance, if you are attempting to copy an object that stores a cache as a dictionary (which might be large), it might not make sense to copy the cache as well -- if the cache can be shared in memory between instances, then it should be.

Pickling Your Objects

If you spend time with other Pythonistas, chances are you've at least heard of pickling. Pickling is a serialization process for Python data structures, and can be incredibly useful when you need to store an object and retrieve it later (usually for caching). It's also a major source of worries and confusion.

Pickling is so important that it doesn't just have its own module (pickle), but its own *protocol* and the magic methods to go with it. But first, a brief word on how to pickle existing types(feel free to skip it if you already know).

Pickling: A Quick Soak in the Brine

Let's dive into pickling. Say you have a dictionary that you want to store and retrieve later. You could write it's contents to a file, carefully making sure that you write correct syntax, then retrieve it using either exec() or processing the file input. But this is precarious at best: if you store important data in plain text, it could be corrupted or changed in any number of ways to make your program crash or worse run malicious code on your computer. Instead, we're going to pickle it:

```
import pickle

data = {'foo': [1, 2, 3],
        'bar': ('Hello', 'world!'),
        'baz': True}
```

```
jar = open('data.pkl', 'wb')
pickle.dump(data, jar) # write the pickled data to the file jar
jar.close()
```

Now, a few hours later, we want it back. All we have to do is unpickle it:

```
import pickle

pkl_file = open('data.pkl', 'rb') # connect to the pickled data
data = pickle.load(pkl_file) # load it into a variable
print data
pkl_file.close()
```

What happens? Exactly what you expect. It's just like we had data all along.

Now, for a word of caution: pickling is not perfect. Pickle files are easily corrupted on accident and on purpose. Pickling may be more secure than using flat text files, but it still can be used to run malicious code. It's also incompatible across versions of Python, so don't expect to distribute pickled objects and expect people to be able to open them. However, it can also be a powerful tool for caching and other common serialization tasks.

Pickling your own Objects

Pickling isn't just for built-in types. It's for any class that follows the pickle protocol. The pickle protocol has four optional methods for Python objects to customize how they act (it's a bit different for C extensions, but that's not in our scope):

__getinitargs__(self)

> If you'd like for __init__ to be called when your class is unpickled, you can define __getinitargs__, which should return a tuple of the arguments that you'd like to be passed to __init__. Note that this method will only work for old-style classes.

__getnewargs__(self)

> For new-style classes, you can influence what arguments get passed to __new__ upon unpickling. This method should also return a tuple of arguments that will then be passed to __new__.

__getstate__(self)

Instead of the object's __dict__ attribute being stored, you can return a custom state to be stored when the object is pickled. That state will be used by __setstate__ when the object is unpickled.

__setstate__(self, state)
When the object is unpickled, if __setstate__ is defined the object's state will be passed to it instead of directly applied to the object's __dict__. This goes hand in hand with __getstate__: when both are defined, you can represent the object's pickled state however you want with whatever you want.

__reduce__(self)
When defining extension types (i.e., types implemented using Python's C API), you have to tell Python how to pickle them if you want them to pickle them. __reduce__() is called when an object defining it is pickled. It can either return a string representing a global name that Python will look up and pickle, or a tuple. The tuple contains between 2 and 5 elements: a callable object that is called to recreate the object, a tuple of arguments for that callable object, state to be passed to __setstate__(optional), an iterator yielding list items to be pickled (optional), and an iterator yielding dictionary items to be pickled (optional).

__reduce_ex__(self)
__reduce_ex__ exists for compatibility. If it is defined, __reduce_ex__ will be called over __reduce__ on pickling. __reduce__ can be defined as well for older versions of the pickling API that did not support __reduce_ex__.

An Example

Our example is a Slate, which remembers what its values have been and when those values were written to it. However, this particular slate goes blank each time it is pickled: the current value will not be saved.

```
import time

class Slate:
    '''Class to store a string and a changelog, and forget its value when
    pickled.'''

    def __init__(self, value):
        self.value = value
        self.last_change = time.asctime()
```

```
    self.history = {}

    def change(self, new_value):
        # Change the value. Commit last value to history
        self.history[self.last_change] = self.value
        self.value = new_value
        self.last_change = time.asctime()

    def print_changes(self):
        print 'Changelog for Slate object:'
        for k, v in self.history.items():
            print '%s\t %s' % (k, v)

    def __getstate__(self):
        # Deliberately do not return self.value or self.last_change.
        # We want to have a "blank slate" when we unpickle.
        return self.history

    def __setstate__(self, state):
        # Make self.history = state and last_change and value undefined
        self.history = state
        self.value, self.last_change = None, None
```

The goal of this chapter is to bring something to anyone that reads it, regardless of their experience with Python or object-oriented programming. If you're just getting started with Python, you've gained valuable knowledge of the basics of writing feature-rich, elegant, and easy-to-use classes. If you're an intermediate Python programmer, you've probably picked up some slick new concepts and strategies and some good ways to reduce the amount of code written by you and clients. If you're an expert Pythonista, you've been refreshed on some of the stuff you might have forgotten about and maybe picked up a few new tricks along the way. Whatever your experience level, I hope that this trip through Python's special methods has been truly magical (I couldn't resist the final pun).

Appendix: How to Call Magic Methods

Some of the magic methods in Python directly map to built-in functions; in this case, how to invoke them is fairly obvious. However, in other cases, the invocation is far less obvious. This appendix is devoted to exposing non-obvious syntax that leads to magic methods getting called.

Magic Method	When it gets invoked (example)	Explanation
__new__(cls [,...])	instance = MyClass(arg1, arg2)	__new__ is called on instance creation
__init__(self [,...])	instance = MyClass(arg1, arg2)	__init__ is called on instance creation
__cmp__(self, other)	self == other, self > other, etc.	Called for any comparison
__pos__(self)	+self	Unary plus sign
__neg__(self)	-self	Unary minus sign
__invert__(self)	~self	Bitwise inversion
__index__(self)	x[self]	Conversion when object is used as index
__nonzero__(self)	bool(self)	Boolean value of the object
__getattr__(self, name)	self.name # name doesn't exist	Accessing nonexistent attribute
__setattr__(self, name, val)	self.name = val	Assigning to an attribute
__delattr__(self, name)	del self.name	Deleting an attribute
__getattribute__(self, name)	self.name	Accessing any attribute
__getitem__(self, key)	self[key]	Accessing an item using an index
__setitem__(self, key, val)	self[key] = val	Assigning to an item using an index
__delitem__(self, key)	del self[key]	Deleting an item using an index
__iter__(self)	for x in self	Iteration
__contains__(self, value)	value in self, value not in self	Membership tests using in
__call__(self [,...])	self(args)	"Calling" an instance
__enter__(self)	with self as x:	with statement context

Magic Method	When it gets invoked (example)	Explanation
		managers
__exit__(self, exc, val, trace)	with self as x:	with statement context managers
__getstate__(self)	pickle.dump(pkl_file, self)	Pickling
__setstate__(self)	data = pickle.load(pkl_file)	Pickling

Hopefully, this table should have cleared up any questions you might have had about what syntax invokes which magic method.